mustsees
Florida
featuring **Orlando**

and Photo: Visit Florida

MICHELIN

mustsees **Florida** featuring **Orlando**

Editorial Manager	Jonathan P. Gilbert
Editor	M. Linda Lee
Writer	Shea R. Dean
Production Manager	Natasha G. George
Cartography	Peter Wrenn
Photo Editor	Yoshimi Kanazawa
Researcher	Glenn Michael Harper
Photo Research	Michelle Bowen
Layout	Michelle Bowen, Natasha G. George
Interior Design	Chris Bell, cbdesign
Cover Design	Chris Bell, cbdesign, Natasha G. George

Contact Us

Michelin Travel and Lifestyle
One Parkway South
Greenville, SC 29615
USA
www.michelintravel.com
michelin.guides@us.michelin.com

Michelin TravelPartner
Hannay House
39 Clarendon Road
Watford, Herts WD17 1JA
UK
(01923) 205 240
www.ViaMichelin.com
travelpubsales@uk.michelin.com

Special Sales

For information regarding bulk sales, customized
editions and premium sales, please contact
our Customer Service Departments:

USA	1-800-432-6277
UK	(01923) 205 240
Canada	1-800-361-8236

Michelin Apa Publications Ltd
A joint venture between Michelin and Langenscheidt

58 Borough High Street, London SE1 1XF, United Kingdom

© 2011 Michelin Apa Publications Ltd
ISBN 978-1-907099-36-6
Printed: August 2011
Printed and bound: Himmer, Germany

Note to the reader:
While every effort is made to ensure that all information printed in this guide is correct and
up-to-date, Michelin Apa Publications Ltd. accepts no liability for any direct, indirect or
consequential losses howsoever caused so far as such can be excluded by law. Admission
prices listed for sights in this guide are for a single adult, unless otherwise specified.

Welcome to Florida

Beach at Islamorada, Florida Keys

Introduction

The Sunshine State 32

Must See

Everglades	**36**
Southern Everglades	39
Northern Everglades	41
Florida Keys	**44**
Islands	46
Museums	48
Historic Sites	49
Miami and South Florida	**52**
Cities	54
Museums	61
Historic Sites	64

p54

Northeast Coast	**74**
Cities	76
Museums	78
Historic Sites	79
Orlando Area	**86**
Cities	87
Theme Parks	88
Excursion	96
The Panhandle	**102**
Cities	104
Museums	106
Historic Sites	107
Southwest Coast	**112**
Cities	114
Museums	117
Historic Sites	120

Must Do

Everglades	**42**
The Great Outdoors	42
Florida Keys	**50**
Animal Parks	50
Shopping	50
The Great Outdoors	51
Miami and South Florida	**66**
Beaches	66
Animal Parks	67
The Great Outdoors	68
Performing Arts	69
Shopping	71
Nightlife	72
Spas	73
Northeast Coast	**82**
Animal Parks	82
Beaches	82
The Great Outdoors	83
Performing Arts	83
Shopping	84
Spas	85
Orlando Area	**97**
The Great Outdoors	97
Performing Arts	98
Shopping	99
Nightlife	100
Spas	101

TABLE OF CONTENTS

p118

The Panhandle	108
Beaches	108
The Great Outdoors	109
Performing Arts	110
Shopping	111
Nightlife	111
Southwest Coast	121
Beaches	121
The Great Outdoors	122
Family Fun	124
Performing Arts	126
Shopping	127
Nightlife	128
Spas	129

Must Eat

| **Restaurants** | 130 |

Must Stay

| **Hotels** | 142 |

Must Know

Star Attractions	6
Ideas and Tours	12
Calendar of Events	16
Practical Information	20
Index	154

p 140

TABLE OF CONTENTS

★★★ ATTRACTIONS

Unmissable historic, cultural and natural sights

MUST KNOW

© Florida Department of Environmental Protection

Dr. Julian G. Bruce St. George
Island State Park   p 108

© Wizreist/Dreamstime.com

Cathedral-Basilica of
St. Augustine   p 80

© Jennifer Mann/Dreamstime.com

Castillo de San Marcos
National Monument   p 79

© Disney

Disney's Hollywood Studios   p 95

Florida Caverns State Park   p 109

South Beach   p 66

The Dalí Museum   p 117

STAR ATTRACTIONS

★★★ ATTRACTIONS

Unmissable historic, cultural and natural sights

For more than 75 years, people have used Michelin stars to take the guesswork out of travel. Our star-rating system helps you make the best decision on where to go, what to do, and what to see.

★★★	Unmissable
★★	Worth a trip
★	Worth a detour
No star	Recommended

★★★Three Star

Art Deco Historic District *p 58*
Castillo de San Marcos Natl Monument *p 79*
The Dalí Museum *p 117*
Disney's Animal Kingdom *p 95*
Disney's Hollywood Studios *p 95*
Epcot *p 93*
Everglades National Park *p 39*
Kennedy Space Center *p 96*
Key West *p 47*
Miami *p 54*
Miami Beach *p 57*
Orlando *p 87*
Palm Beach *p 58*
SeaWorld Orlando *p 88*
South Beach *p 66*
St. Augustine *p 76*
Universal Orlando *p 90*
Vizcaya *p 64*
Walt Disney World Resort *p 92*

★★Two Star

Amelia Island *p 82*
Ancient Spanish Monastery *p 64*
Anhinga Trail *p 49*
Bahia Honda State Park *p 51*

Barnacle State Historic Park *p 64*
Big Cypress Bend *p 42*
Bok Tower Gardens National Historic Landmark *p 97*
Busch Gardens *p 124*
Cathedral-Basilica of St. Augustine *p 80*
Coconut Grove *p 56*
Coral Gables *p 56*
Cruises of Ten Thousand Islands *p 42*
Dr. Julian G. Bruce St. George Island State Park *p 108*
Cummer Museum of Art and Gardens *p 78*
Ernest Hemingway Home and Museum *p 49*
Everglades boat cruises *p 40*
Fairchild Tropical Garden *p 68*
Flagler Museum *p 61*
Florida Caverns State Park *p 109*
Fort Clinch State Park *p 80*
Fort Matanzas National Momument *p 80*
Gonzalez-Alvarez House *p 80*
Grayton Beach State Park *p 108*

Harry S Truman Little White House Museum *p 49*
HistoryMiami *p 61*
Hyde Park *p 116*
J.N. "Ding" Darling NWR *p 122*
John and Mable Ringling Museum of Art *p 117*
John Pennekamp Coral Reef State Park *p 51*
Lion Country Safari *p 67*
Marie Selby Botanical Gardens *p 122*
Museum of Arts and Sciences *p 79*
Museum of Discovery and Science *p 61*
Museum of Fine Arts *p 118*
Museum of Science & Industry *p 119*
Myakka River State Park *p 123*
National Museum of Naval Aviation *p 106*
Norton Museum of Art *p 62*
Ocean Drive *p 58*
Old Town, Key West *p 47*
Pa-hay-okee Overlook *p 40*
Sanibel and Captiva Islands *p 121*
Shark Valley *p 41*

Sarasota *p 114*
Southern Everglades
  Driving Tour *p 39*
St. Petersburg *p 114*
Tampa *p 115*
Upper and Middle
  Keys *p 46*
Venetian Pool *p 68*
Wakulla Springs
  State Park *p 109*
Wolfsonian – FIU *p 62*
Worth Avenue *p 71*
Ximenez-Fatio
  House *p 81*
Zoo Miami *p 67*

★One Star

Apalachicola *p 104*
Arthur R. Marshall
  Loxahatchee
  NWR *p 68*
Audubon House
  and Tropical
  Gardens *p 49*
Bass Museum
  of Art *p 62*
Bayside Marketplace
  p 55, 71
Bill Baggs Cape
  Florida State Park
  p 66
Biscayne National
  Park *p 68*
Boca Raton *p 59*
Boca Raton Museum
  of Art *p 62*
Bonnet House
  Museum and
  Gardens *p 65*
Butterfly World *p 67*
Coconut Grove
  Village *p 57*
Colonial Spanish
  Quarter *p 81*
Coral Castle *p 65*
Cracker Creek
  Canoeing *p 83*

Crane Point Museums
  and Nature Point
  p 48
Delnor-Wiggins Pass
  State Park *p 121*
Dolphin Research
  Center *p 50*
Dow Museum of
  Historic Houses *p 81*
Dry Tortugas National
  Park *p 51*
Eco Pond *p 40*
Edison and Ford
  Winter Estates *p 120*
Fakahatchee
  Strand Preserve
  State Park *p 42*
Florida Aquarium
  p 125
Fort De Soto Park
  p 121
Fort Lauderdale *p 60*
Fort Pickens *p 107*
Goodwood Museum
  & Gardens *p 107*
Government House
  Museum *p 81*
Gumbo Limbo
  Trail *p 39*
Harry P. Leu
  Gardens *p 97*
Henry B. Plant
  Museum *p 119*
Historic Spanish
  Point *p 120*
Jacksonville Zoo *p 82*
Jungle Island *p 67*
Lovers Key
  State Park *p 121*
Lowe Art
  Museum *p 62*
Lower Keys *p 47*
Maclay Gardens
  State Park *p 109*
Mel Fisher Maritime
  Heritage Society
  p 48

Miami Art
  Museum *p 63*
Mission San Luis *p 107*
Morikami Museum
  and Japanese
  Gardens *p 63*
Museum of Art, Fort
  Lauderdale *p 63*
Museum of
  Contemporary Art
  p 63
Museum of Florida
  History *p 106*
Museum of Science
  and History and
  Planetarium *p 79*
Naples *p 116*
Naples Museum
  of Art *p 119*
National Key Deer
  Refuge *p 51*
Palofax Historic
  Distric *p 105*
Park Avenue Historic
  District *p 105*
Pensacola *p 104*
Ponce de Leon Inlet
  Lighthouse *p 77*
Shark Valley Tram
  Tour *p 41*
St. Andrews State
  Park *p 108*
St. Augustine
  Alligator Farm
  Zoological Park *p 82*
Stranahan House *p 65*
The Strip *p 66*
Tallahassee *p 105*
Tallahassee Museum
  of History Natural
  Science *p 106*
Theater of
  the Sea *p 48*
Timucuan Ecological
  and Historic Natl
  Preserve *p 81*
West Lake Trail *p 40*

STAR ATTRACTIONS

ACTIVITIES

Unmissable activities and entertainment

Swim in the Venetian Pool   p 68

Watch the sunset   p 47

Slurp oysters in Apalachicola
p 104

Encounter a dolphin   p 15

MUST KNOW

QUINTESSENTIAL FLORIDA

Unmissable activities, entertainment, restaurants and hotels
For every historic and natural sight in Florida, there are a thousand other ways you can have fun. We recommend all of the activities in this guide, but our top picks are highlighted with the Michelin Man logo.

Outings

Drive through the Southern Everglades *p 39*
Take a cruise of the Ten Thousand Islands *p 42*
Spend a day at Bahia Honda State Park *p 51*
Watch the sunset *p 47*
Encounter a dolphin *p 15*
Visit a Disney classic *p 92*
Meet Harry Potter and his friends *p 91*
Take a safari *p 95*
See a space shuttle *p 96*
Fly a virtual fighter plane *p 106*
Climb colonial-era ramparts *p 79*
See a miniature circus *p 118*

Hotels

Marquesa Hotel *p 144*
Biltmore Hotel *p 146*
The Breakers *p 146*
Hotel Place St. Michel *p 145*
Delano *p 146*
The Courtyard at Lake Lucerne *p 148*
Disney's Animal Kingdom Lodge *p 149*
New World Inn *p 150*
Safety Harbor Resort and Spa *p 151*
St. Francis Inn *p 148*
'Tween Waters Inn *p 153*

Nightlife

Party in Key West *p 48*
Take the Fernandina Pub Crawl *p 85*
Check out the action on Church Street *p 100*
Southern blues *p 111*

Relax

Have a café cubano in Little Havana *p 55*
Chill on Ocean Drive *p 58*
Party on The Strip in Fort Lauderdale *p 66*
Swim in the Venetian Pool *p 68*
Attend a concert at the New World Center *p 70*
Slurp oysters in Apalachicola *p 104*
Hunt for shells on Sanibel Island *p 121*

Restaurants

Blue Heaven *p 131*
Joe's Stone Crab *p 133*
Cuban food at Café Versailles *p 133*
News Café for the scene *p 132*
Café Gala for tapas *p 117*
San Angel Inn *p 136*
Victoria and Albert's *p 137*
Columbia Restaurant *p 139*
Wine list at Bern's Steak House *p 141*
Marina Café *p 138*

Shopping

Mouse ears and Disney souvenirs *p 99*
High-end designer clothes *p 71*
Beachwear *p 127*
Cigars *p 115*
Designer boutiques *p 127*
Art galleries *p 71*
Antiques *p 84*
Outlets *p 99*

Sports

Watch a football game *p 69*
See the Daytona 500 *p 78*
Canoe the Myakka River *p 122*
MLB spring training *p 123*
Fish from St. Pete's Pier *p 114*
Snorkel and scuba dive *p 51*

STAR ATTRACTIONS

IDEAS AND TOURS

Throughout this thematic guide, you will find inspiration for a thousand different ways to spend your time in Florida. The following is a selection of ideas to start you off. *Sites in bold can be found in the Index.*

BOAT TOURS

Since Florida boasts 1,200mi of coastline, it would be a shame to visit the state and not get out on the water. Here are some suggestions of ways to do just that.

Cruises of Ten Thousand Islands★★

Everglades City is the departure point for this popular boat tour, which reveals the marine world of **Chokoloskee Bay** in the **Everglades★★★**. Another option, the **mangrove wilderness tour**, explores the park's swamps on a six-passenger boat.

Boat Tours of Biscayne Bay

A great way to see Miami from the water and admire the city's stunning coastline is via a boat cruise on Biscayne Bay *(www.miamitours.us)*. En route, you'll see the Port of Miami; Palm Island, once home to gangster Al Capone; and "millionaire's row" on Miami Beach.

🚗 DRIVING TOURS

You can carve a driving tour out of innumerable routes through the Sunshine State, but these are a couple of highlights.

Ocean Boulevard, Palm Beach

A drive along **Ocean Boulevard** in **Palm Beach★★★**, from Southern Boulevard to Barton Avenue, will take you past some of the most luxurious estates on the Florida coast. At Barton Avenue, continue one block west to glimpse **Bethesda-by-the-Sea★★**, a charming Gothic Revival stone church.

MUST KNOW

Alligator, Everglades National Park

© 2008 Richard Nowitz/Apa Publications

Southern Everglades

The **Everglades★★★** have been designated a World Heritage Site, an International Biosphere Reserve, and a Wetland of International Importance. Attractions in the southern part of **Everglades National Park★★★** are organized as a 38mi driving tour, which starts at **Coe Visitor Center** (11mi southwest of Homestead) and ends at **Flamingo**, the jumping-off point for boat tours and other excursions in the park.

⏳WALKING TOURS
Art Deco Historic District★★★

The **Miami Design Preservation League** offers several guided tours that take in some of the myriad Art Deco structures that lie within the one-square-mile district. A good introduction is the 90-minute walking tour that reveals a number of the building's interiors as well. All tours depart from the **Art Deco Welcome Center** *(1001 Ocean Dr. at 10th St.; www.mdpl.org)*.

Key West★★★

Take a walking tour through Old Town Key West, where you'll see some impressive architecture, including the simple wood-framed conch houses, which mimic those built by the island's 19C Bahamian settlers. Begin at Mallory Square, and make your way up Duval Street, detouring along Caroline, Simonton and Eaton streets.

Ybor City★

While you're in **Tampa★★**, take time to discover the rich history of Ybor City as you stroll along **Seventh Avenue★**, the heart of this Latino district. Be sure to

Shell Island, Florida

Photo Courtesy of Vist Florida

stop for a cup of *café cubano* and perhaps a hand-rolled cigar. Tours, which start at **Centro Ybor** *(corner of 17th St. and 9th Ave.)* are conducted by Ybor City Historic Walking Tours *(www.ybor walkingtours.com)*.

ISLAND HOPPING

In Florida, island excursions range from popular resort communities to remote tranquil islets.

Shell Island★★

Take a ferry from **St. Andrews State Park★** at the end of Panama City Beach to reach this unspoiled barrier island in the Gulf of Mexico. Here you'll find shells galore and peace and quiet on a stretch of sparkling white sand.

Dry Tortugas National Park★

You'll have to take a plane or a boat to reach this national park, which sits in the Gulf of Mexico, about 69mi southwest of Key West. Encompassing 100sq mi, the park protects the small cluster of reef islands called the Dry Tortugas. It's worth boarding a plane or boat

13

for the trip over to 10-acre Garden Key, where you can tour the site of the 19C military installation **Fort Jefferson** (see p 51).

Anna Maria Island

You can drive to this laid-back Gulf Coast barrier island, north of **Sarasota★★**. On the island's southern end, lovely Coquina Beach provides picnic tables, a café, a playground and turquoise Gulf waters for swimming.

Cabbage Key

For a real getaway, board a boat to this tiny island, 8mi north of **Sanibel and Captiva Islands★★**. There are no paved roads (and no cars allowed) on Cabbage Key, but there is a small inn (built in 1938) where you can stay and eat while you escape civilization.

Sea Islands

You won't have to take a boat to reach the Sea Isands off the coast of Jacksonville. **Amelia Island★★**, with its tony all-inclusive resorts and 13 miles of beaches, is probably the best known. Then there's **Fort George Island★**, site of the **Timucuan Ecological and Historical National Preserve★**. Just east of Fort George Island is

Timucuan Ecological and Historical National Preserve

Photo Courtesy of Visit Florida

Little Talbot Island with its state park, hiking trails and pristine beaches.

OUTDOOR ACTIVITIES
Snorkel in John Pennekamp Coral Reef State Park★★

Located in **Key Largo★**, the country's first underwater state park provides access to 70 nautical miles of the **Florida Reef★★★**, the largest living coral reef system in North America. Don a snorkel mask and fins to explore the reef, or bring your scuba gear for an even closer look at the denizens of this underwater world. Park rangers lead 2.5-hour snorkeling tours.

Bike through a Wildlife Refuge

Set at the northernmost tip of the Everglades, the **Arthur R. Marshall Loxahatchee National Wildlife Refuge★** is home to a host of wildlife, including some 180,000 alligators, 24 kinds of snakes and 257 species of birds. For an overview, bike along the 12mi trail that begins at the park headquarters.

Canoe the Wilderness Waterway

This inland course traces the waterways for 99mi along protected rivers and bays from Everglades City to Flamingo in **Everglades National Park★★★**. Ply these waters on your own by motorboat (6–8hrs) or by canoe (a trip that takes 8–10 days).

Explore a Cave

The only state park in Florida to offer cave tours, **Florida Caverns State Park★★** in Marianna takes visitors through a dazzling cave system, for an up-close view of some impressive limestone formations *(no tours Tue or Wed)*. The park also has facilities for camping, canoeing, kayaking and biking.

WILDLIFE ENCOUNTERS
National Key Deer Refuge★
While a trip to this National Wildlife Refuge on Big Pine Key doesn't guarantee an encounter with the protected species of tiny (2ft at the shoulder) deer, this is the best place to see them. Take one of the two trails through the preserved habitat at dusk or dawn, and you'll have a good chance of spotting some of these tiny creatures.

⚓ Swim with Dolphins
SeaWorld Orlando★★★ – This marine park offers an opportunity to meet dolphins. Sign up for the 45-minute **Dolphins Up-Close Tour** (*additional fee*) at **Dolphin Cove**, and you'll get to visit the dolphin nursery and interact with dolphins as part of a training session, led by member of SeaWorld's Animal Care staff.
Dolphin Research Center★ – On your way down to Key West, stop in at the Dolphin Research Center on Grassy Key, where you can sign up for a special dolphin-encounter program. Options range from being trainer for a day to 20 minutes of time in the water with these fascinating mammals.
Theater of the Sea★ – At this marine park on Windley Key, not only can you get in the water with dolphins, but Theater of the Sea offers programs where visitors

can swim with docile southern stingrays and frolic with playful sea lions in a saltwater lagoon.

Quick Trips
Stuck for ideas? Try these:

Animal Parks *50, 67, 82*
Animal Safaris *67, 95*
Antiques Shopping *84*
Aquariums *88, 125*
Art Deco Architecture *58*
Art Museums *62, 63, 78, 117, 119*
Beaches *66, 77, 82, 108, 121*
Bird-watching *39, 42, 43*
Boating *42, 83*
Cuisine *130*
Daytona 500 *17, 78*
Family Fun *124*
Festivals *16*
Football Games *69, 123*
Gardens *68, 97, 122, 123*
Historic Sites *49, 64, 79, 107, 120*
History Museums *61, 79, 81, 106, 119*
Islands *46, 121*
Latino Districts *55, 115*
National Parks *36, 51, 68, 81*
Natural History Museums *48*
Nightlife *48, 72, 85, 100, 111, 128*
Performing Arts *69, 83, 98, 110, 126*
Outlet Shopping *99*
Resort Hotels *143*
Science Museums *61, 79, 119*
Shopping in Key West *50*
Snorkeling *51*
Spa Day *73, 85, 101, 129*
Space Center *96*
Spanish Colonial Sites *81*
Spring Training *123*
State Parks *51, 80, 109, 123*
Sunset Celebration *47*
Swanky Shopping *60, 71, 127*
Theme Park Nightlife *100*
Theme Park Shopping *99*
Theme Parks *88*
Thrill Rides *89, 90, 95*
Wildlife Refuges *42, 43, 68, 122*

IDEAS AND TOURS

CALENDAR OF EVENTS

Listed below is a selection of Florida's most popular annual events; some dates may vary from year to year. For detailed information on these and other festivals, contact local tourism offices (numbers listed under individual entries) or Visit Florida *(850-488-5607 or 888-735-2872; www.visitflorida.com)*.

January

Bowl games

New Year's Day is prime time for college football, and no less than four major bowl (arena) games are played in Florida that day, pitting some of the best teams in the country against one another. Games include the **Discover Orange Bowl in Miami** *(www.orangebowl.org)*, the **Gator Bowl** in Jacksonville *(www.gatorbowl.com)*, the **Outback Bowl** *(www.outback bowl.com)* held in Tampa, and Orlando's **Capital One Bowl** *(www.capitalonebowl.com)*.

Art Deco Weekend

More than 85 events draw upwards of 300,000 people to celebrate Miami Beach's vaunted Art Deco architecture and legacy. Arts and crafts fairs, guided tours, films, lectures, even a dog parade are in the offing *(mid-Jan; 305-672-2014; www.mdpl.org)*.

Miami International Art Fair

Though it's only been on the scene for a few years, this Miami Beach art fair has become one of the hottest in the world, with thousands of dealers, artists and collectors coming together to show off and hobnob *(mid-Jan; www.mia-artfair.com)*.

Gasparilla Pirate Fest

Ahoy, mateys! This major festival fills the streets of Tampa with live entertainment, food vendors and, of course, plenty of swashbuckling pirates in a massive parade *(late Jan; gasparillapiratefest.com)*.

ING Miami Marathon

Founded in 2003, this 26.2-mile race now brings more than 20,000 runners from every state and nearly 80 countries to wend their way through the streets of Miami, Miami Beach, and Coconut Grove. A half-marathon is run simultaneously *(late Jan; www.ingmiamimarathon.com)*.

February

Florida State Fair

Visiting the coast, you might forget that Florida is a major agricultural state. Come to Tampa for a fun-filled reminder, complete with livestock judging competitions, carnival rides, arts and crafts and entertainment *(12 days in mid-Feb; 813-621-7821; www.floridastatefair.com)*.

February Daytona 500

Photo Courtesy of Visit Florida

Coconut Grove Arts Festival

Nearly 50 years old, this celebrated arts festival attracts 350 artists to show their wares along the historic streets of Coconut Grove in Miami. As you browse you'll be privy to live entertainment and fine food as well *(mid-Feb; 305-447-0401; www.coconutgroveartsfest.com)*.

Daytona 500

The most prestigious NASCAR race in the country draws more than 100,000 fans – as well as an A-list of music stars to sing the national anthem – to watch 43 cars zoom around the storied 2.5 mile track in Daytona Beach some 200 times. Show up early for the tailgating party *(late Feb; 866-990-7223; www.daytona internationalspeedway.com)*.

March
Carnaval Miami

Calle Ocho from 12th to 27th Avenues is transformed into a major street party, with dancing, music, food, arts, children's activities, and – of course – spectacle, as locals don their most outrageous and revealing outfits *(late Feb-early Mar; 305-644-8888; www.carnavalmiami.com)*.

Florida Strawberry Festival

Plant City, a town of 30,000 on the outskirts of Tampa, calls itself the strawberry capital of the world; and at this down-home spring festival it proves it with carnival rides, a beauty pageant, livestock displays, and entertainment by such big names as .38 Special and Kenny Rogers. There's plenty of strawberry shortcake to go around *(12 days in early Mar; 813-752-9194; www.flstrawberryfestival.com)*.

Bike Week Daytona

Thousands of motorcycle enthusiasts rumble into town for ten days for an annual rally featuring a Clydesdale parade (courtesy of Budweiser, an event sponsor), merchandise fairs, raffles, and races at the Daytona International Speedway *(early Mar; www.officialbike week.com)*.

April
Springtime Tallahassee

A grand parade, more than 200 arts and crafts vendors, three entertainment stages, a children's area, seafood and a beer garden mark this Tallahassee festival, which has been going strong since the late 1960s *(late Mar or early Apr; www. springtimetallahassee.com)*.

Fun 'N Sun Festival

Big names in jazz, country and blues turn out to entertain at the popular concert season in Clearwater, which kicks off with a street party *(late Apr–early May; 727- 562-4700; www.clear water-fl.com)*.

May
SunFest

This weekend-long festival attracts more than 250,000 revelers to Flagler Drive in downtown West Palm Beach for a juried arts and crafts show, food, drinks and entertainment that includes a fierce battle of the bands. It concludes with fireworks *(early May; 561-659-5980; www.sunfest.com)*.

Isle of Eight Flags Shrimp Festival

Kicking off with a pirate parade in Fernandina Beach, the annual weekend fest continues with sidewalk sales, a kids' fun zone, a beauty pageant, 450 fine arts and crafts vendors, music concerts, fireworks and, of course, plenty of shrimp to eat *(early May; 904-261-5841; www.shrimpfestival.com)*.

Florida Folk Festival

This three-day celebration over Memorial Day weekend has been going strong in White Springs for nearly sixty years. There's plenty of music as well as Irish dancing, storytelling, regional food (kumquat pie!), and how-to workshops on everything from basket weaving to playing the mandolin *(late May; 877-635-3655; www.floridafolkfestival.com)*.

Jacksonville Jazz Festival

Free performances from some of the biggest names in jazz (Natalie Cole, John Pizzarelli, Eddie Palmieri) are the highlight of this Memorial Day weekend street fest, which also includes wine and craft brew tastings, a juried art show and a jazz piano competition *(late May; 904-630-3686; www.jaxjazzfest.com)*.

June

Billy Bowlegs Festival

Bring your eye patch and your Jolly Roger to Fort Walton Beach for this spirited pirate-themed festival, featuring a pet parade, a treasure hunt, a pub crawl, live music and theater, storytelling, fireworks and more *(early Jun; www.billybowlegsfestival.com)*.

Goombay Festival

Celebrating Miami's ties to the Caribbean, the Bahamian festival peaks with a traditional parade of brightly costumed dancers gyrating to the percussive rhythms of drums and cowbells. Food vendors cooking up both American and Bahamian cuisine line the route in Coconut Grove *(early June; 305-448-9501; www.goombayfestivalcoconut grove.com)*.

Sarasota Music Festival

Fifty-eight of the finest young classical musicians in the world join 40 guest artists in Sarasota for three weeks each year to study and perform chamber music.

SunFest, West Palm Beach

Photo Courtesy of Visit Florida

Members of the public are invited to attend artist showcases, master classes, concerts, and lectures for a very reasonable price *(early-mid Jun; 941-953-3434; www.sarasotaorchestra.org; Sarasota)*.

July
Hemingway Days
Burly, white-bearded men come out of the Key West's brightly painted woodwork to compete in the look-alike contest that's part of this annual celebration of Hemingway's time on the island. Literary events, a mock running of the bulls, and a marlin tournament are also scheduled *(mid-July; www.fla-keys.com)*.

September
Destin Seafood Festival
This harborside festival has live music, arts and crafts vendors, and deliciously fresh *fruits de mer* prepared by local restaurants *(late Sept–early Oct; www.destin chamber.com)*.

October
Clearwater Jazz Holiday
This major jazz festival spans four days and four nights, presenting a mix of smooth jazz, R&B, Latin jazz and fusion. Past fests have drawn the likes of Tony Bennett, Stan Getz, and Tito Puente as headliners *(mid-Oct; 727-461-5200; www.clearwaterjazz.com)*.

John's Pass Seafood Festival
Live music, craft vendors, a fishing expo, a children's Halloween costume contest, and seafood galore mark this annual festival in Madeira Beach *(late Oct; www.johnspass.com)*.

Fantasy Fest
A mile-long stretch of Key West's Duval Street hosts an "eater-tainment extravaganza" as part of this gay and lesbian festival, with costumed merrymakers, food and drink, arts and crafts, and music *(late Oct; www.fantasyfest.net)*.

November
Florida Seafood Festival
Nearly three-quarters of the oysters harvested in Florida come from Apalachicola Bay. Hence, two fiercely competitive contests in Apalachicola—oyster eating and oyster shucking—are the centerpiece of a program that also includes a parade, a blessing of the fleet and a 5K run *(early Nov; 888-653-8011; www.floridaseafoodfestival.com)*.

December
Winterfest Boat Parade
In what has become one of the biggest parades in the country, a nightly flotilla of brightly illuminated yachts travels a 12-mile course through Fort Lauderdale, watched by some one million spectators. There's also a family fun day, a black tie ball, and a golf and tennis competition *(early Dec; www.winterfestparade.com)*.

King Mango Strut
This campy parade through Miami's Coconut Grove was born in 1981, when its founders were barred from playing kazoos and banging on garbage cans in the Orange Bowl Parade. That parade is no longer, but the King Mango Strut lives on, mixing humor and protest in hilarious fashion *(late Dec; www.kingmangostrut.org)*.

CALENDAR OF EVENTS

PRACTICAL INFORMATION

WHEN TO GO

A year-round destination, the Sunshine State has no real off-season. Most sights and attractions are open year-round, although peak seasons vary by region. High season in south Florida is during the **winter** (*Oct–Apr*), when many visitors come to escape colder climates.

Daytime winter temperatures in Miami average 68°F/20°C, while in the Everglades and Keys, daytime temperatures can rise to 73°F/23°C. North and central Florida enjoy the traditional four seasons: spring 67°F/19°C; summer 83°F/29°C; fall 69°F/21°C; and winter 55°F/14°C. January is typically the coldest month.

Throughout Florida, the **summer** months (*May–Sept*) see the highest humidity, and afternoon thundershowers are common. Along the coasts, however, sea breezes do moderate the temperatures somewhat. Daytime

temperatures in summer average 88°F/31°C and do not vary much between the northern and southern regions. Be sure to bring lightweight, comfortable clothing, a hat, insect repellant, sunglasses and sunscreen.

Theme parks are busiest during summer, Christmas and spring holidays. Winter, when mosquitoes are tolerable and migratory birds are plentiful, is the best time to view wildlife in parks and reserves. The **hurricane season** is generally June to November, with the greatest activity occurring from August to October (*see sidebar, p 31*).

Water temperatures are typically warm and pleasant year-round. **Beaches** are most crowded during school holidays, spring breaks and summer vacation periods. Casual dress is accepted in most facilities. Better restaurants may request that men wear jackets, but rarely is a tie required.

Average Daily Temperatures in Florida				
	Jan	**Apr**	**Jul**	**Oct**
Jacksonville	53°F/12°C	69°F/21°C	82°F/28°C	70°F/21°C
Key West	69°F/21°C	78°F/26°C	84°F/29°C	80°F/27°C
Miami	68°F/20°C	76°F/24°C	83°F/29°C	78°F/26°C
Naples	65°F/19°C	73°F/23°C	82°F/28°C	77°F/25°C
Orlando	61°F/16°C	72°F/22°C	83°F/29°C	74°F/23°C
Pensacola	51°F/11°C	68°F/20°C	83°F/29°C	69°F/21°C
Sarasota	60°F/16°C	72°F/22°C	83°F/29°C	75°F/24°C
Tallahassee	51°F/10°C	68°F/20°C	82°F/28°C	68°F/20°C
Tampa	60°F/16°C	68°F/20°C	83°F/29°C	74°F/23°C

MUST KNOW

KNOW BEFORE YOU GO
Useful Websites

www.visitflorida.com – The comprehensive site for all things Florida.

www.myflorida.com – General information for the State of Florida.

www.flheritage.com – State Office of Cultural and Historical Programs; information includes archeology and museum news; arts, and cultural resources.

www.floridastateparks.org – Information on features, fees and reservations at Florida's state parks.

www.see-florida.com – Attractions, lodgings, dining and recreation.

www.accuweather.com – Independent weather-forecasting service, and an excellent source of hurricane information.

www.flasports.com – Site for the Florida Sports Foundation, which is based in Tallahassee.

www.floridacamping.com – Information about Florida RV Parks and campgrounds.

www.dot.state.fl.us – Information from the Florida Department of Transportation.

Tourism Offices

For a copy of the *Florida Vacation Guide* (published annually) or a state map, contact:
VISIT FLORIDA, P.O. Box 1100, Tallahassee FL 32302; *850-488-5607 or 888-735-2872; www visitflorida.com.*
Local tourist offices listed below provide information free of charge on accommodations, shopping, entertainment, festivals and recreation.
Daytona Beach Area Convention & Visitors Bureau – 126 E. Orange Ave., Daytona Beach, FL 32114.

386-255-0415; www.daytona beachcvb.org.

Discover the Palm Beaches of Florida & Boca Raton – 1555 Palm Beach Lakes Blvd., Suite 800, West Palm Beach, FL 33401. *800-554-7256; www.palmbeachfl.com.*

Everglades National Park – 40001 State Road 933, Homestead, FL 33034. *305-242-7700; www.nps. gov/ever.*

Greater Fort Lauderdale Convention & Visitors Bureau – 100 E. Broward Bvld., Suite 200, Fort Lauderdale, FL 33301. *954-765-4466 or 800-22-SUNNY; www.sunny.org.*

The Florida Keys & Key West – *800-352-5397; www.fla-keys.com.*

Visit Jacksonville – 208 N. Laura St., Suite 102, Jacksonville, FL 32202. *904-798-9111or 800-733-2668; www.visitjacksonville.com.*

Lee County Visitors & Convention Bureau /Beaches of Fort Myers & Sanibel – 12800 University Dr., #550, Fort Meyers, FL 33907. *239-338-3500; www.FortMyersSanibel.com.*

Greater Miami Convention & Visitors Bureau – 701 Brickell Ave.,

Photo Courtesy of Visit Florida

Fort Caroline National Memorial, Jacksonville

Suite 2700, Miami, FL 33131. *305-539-3000 or 800-933-8448; www.miamiandbeaches.com.*
Naples, Marco Island, Everglades Convention & Visitors Bureau – 2800 Horseshoe Dr., Naples, FL 34104. *239-252-2384 or 800-688-3600; www.paradisecoast.com.*
Visit Orlando – 8723 International Dr., Suite 101, Orlando, FL 32819. *407-363-5872 or 800-972-3304; www.visitorlando.com.*
Visit Pensacola – 1401 E. Gregory St., Pensacola FL 32502. *800-874-1234; www.visitpensacola.com.*
Sarasota and Her Islands – 701 N. Tamiami Trail, Sarasota, FL 34236. *800-800-3906; www.sarasotafl.org.*
St. Augustine, Ponte Vedra & The Beaches Visitors & Convention Bureau – 29 Old Mission Ave., St. Augustine, FL 32084. *800-653-2489; www.floridashistoriccoast.com.*
St. Petersburg/Clearwater Area Convention & Visitors Bureau – 3805 58th St. N., Suite 2-200, Clearwater, Fl 33760. *727-464-7200 or 877-352-3224. www.visitstpeteclearwater.com.*
Visit Tallahassee – 106 E. Jefferson St., Tallahassee, FL 32301. *850-606-2305 or 800-628-2866; www.visittallahassee.com.*
Tampa Bay & Company – 401 E. Jackson St., Suite 2100, Tampa, FL 33602. *813-223-1111; www.visittampabay.com.*

International Visitors
Foreign Embassies in North America
In addition to the tourism offices throughout Florida, visitors from outside the US can obtain information in French, German, Japanese, Portuguese and Spanish from the website of **Visit Florida** (*www.flausa.com*), or from the US embassy or consulate in their country of residence (*partial listing follows*). For a complete list of American consulates and embassies abroad, visit the US State Department Bureau of Consular Affairs listing online at: *travel. state.gov.* Many foreign countries have consular offices in Miami; for phone numbers, check the Yellow Pages telephone directory under "Consulates").

US Embassies Abroad
Belgium – 27, boulevard du Régent, 1000 Brussels; *02 508-2111; belgium.usembassy.gov.*

Seashells for sale, Florida Keys

Canada – 490 Sussex Drive, Ottawa, Ontario K1N 1G8; *613-688-5335; canada.usembassy.gov.*
Germany – Clayallee 170, 14191 Berlin; *30 238 3050; germany.usembassy.gov.*
Japan – 10-5 Akasaka 1-Chome, Minato-ku Tokyo 107-8420; *03-3224-5000; tokyo.usembassy.gov.*
Switzerland – Sulgeneckstrasse 19, 3007 Bern; 31 357 7011.
United Kingdom – 24 Grosvenor Square, London W1A 1AE; *207 499 9000.*

Entry Requirements

Citizens of countries participating in the **Visa Waiver Pilot Program** (VWPP) are not required to obtain a visa to enter the US for visits of less than 90 days if they have a machine-readable passport. Residents of visa-waiver countries must apply ahead for travel authorization online through the **ESTA program** *(www.cbp.gov/esta)*. Travelers may apply any time before their travel; at least three days before departure is strongly recommended. Citizens of non-participating countries must have a visitor's visa. Upon entry, non-resident foreign visitors – including Canadians – must present a valid passport and round-trip transportation ticket. Naturalized Canadian citizens should carry their citizenship papers.

Air travelers between the US and Canada, Mexico, Central and South America, the Caribbean and Bermuda are also required to present a passport, Air NEXUS card or comparable documentation. All persons traveling between the US and destinations listed above, by land or by sea (including ferry), may be required to present a valid

Florida State Capitol

passport or other documentation, as determined by the US Department of Homeland Security.
Inoculations are generally not required to enter the US, but check with the US embassy or consulate before departing.

Customs Regulations

All articles brought into the US must be declared at time of entry.
Items exempt from customs regulations: personal effects; 150 milliliters (5 fl oz) of alcoholic beverage (providing visitor is at least 21 years old); 150 milliliters (5 fl oz) of perfume containing alcohol; 50 cigarettes and 10 cigars; and gifts (to persons in the US) that do not exceed $200 in value.
Prohibited items include plant material, firearms and ammunition (if not intended for sporting purposes), and meat and poultry products.
For other prohibited items, exemptions and information, contact the **US Customs Service**, 1300 Pennsylvania Ave. N.W., Washington, DC 20229 *(202-354-1000; www.cbp.gov).*

PRACTICAL INFORMATION

Health

The US does not have a national health program that covers foreign nationals. Before departing, visitors from abroad should check their health-care insurance to determine if doctors' visits, medication and hospitalization in the US are covered. Prescription drugs should be properly identified and accompanied by a copy of the prescription. Hotel staff can make recommendations for doctors and other medical services.

Travel Insurance

Companies offering travel insurance within the US include: **Access America** – *(800-284-8300; www.accessamerica.com)*; **Travelex** – *(800-228-9792; www.travelex-insurance.com)*; and **Travel Insured International** – *(800-243-3174; www.travel insured.com)*.

GETTING THERE
By Air

Most US airlines offer direct and non-stop flights to Florida. For flight information, contact the airline directly. Twelve **international airports**—the largest are **Miami**, **Orlando** and **Tampa International**—offer services between Florida and Europe, Central and South America and the Caribbean.
Smaller **regional airports** are usually accessible through commuter carriers. You might get a better airfare deal if you fly into one of the smaller airports; or use a **discount carrier**, such as AirTran, JetBlue and Southwest, who fly in and out of airports in Fort Lauderdale, Fort Myers and West Palm Beach.

By Train

The **Amtrak rail network** offers various train-travel packages that may combine rail, air and bus. Advance reservations are recommended. First-class, coach and sleeping cars are available; on some routes, bi-level Superliner cars with floor-to-ceiling windows afford panoramic views. Canadian travelers should inquire with local travel agents regarding Amtrak/VIARail connections.
The **USA RailPass** (*not available to US or Canadian citizens, or legal residents*) offers unlimited travel within Amtrak-designated regions at discounted rates: Passes are available in three travel durations and segments (15 days/8 segments, 30 days/12 segments, 45 days/18 segments) throughout the US.
The **Auto Train** travels non-stop from Sanford, in central Florida, to Lorton, Virginia (*17mi south of Washington, DC*).
It offers first-class sleeping accommodations, a full-service restaurant, floor-to-ceiling windows in the Sightseer Lounge and a movie presentation, all included in the ticket price *(www.amtrak.com)*.

By Car

Most car travelers enter the Sunshine State via one of two major north-to-south interstate highways: I-95, running along Florida's east coast, from just north of Jacksonville to Miami; and I-75, which enters the state north of Gainesville, and swings toward the west coast, ending in Fort Lauderdale. I-10 runs west to east across the Panhandle and continues on to California.

MUST KNOW

By Bus

Greyhound offers access to most cities in Florida. The Discovery Pass allows unlimited travel anywhere for 7, 15, 30 or 60 days. Advance reservations recommended. For fares, schedules and routes: *800-231-2222; www.discoverypass.com.*

GETTING AROUND
By Car

Distances in Florida are relatively short; it only takes a couple of hours to travel between the east and west coasts (except in the northern part of the state). Even the stretch from the Panhandle to Miami can be driven in a day. For information, contact **Florida Department of Transportation** *(850-414-4100; www.dot.state.fl.us).* Florida has an extensive system of well-maintained major roads. Four major interstates traverse Florida: I-10 runs from Jacksonville to Pensacola and beyond; I-4 links Daytona Beach and Tampa; I-75 cuts southwest across the state from Georgia; and I-95 travels the length of Florida's east coast, ending at Miami. The **Florida Turnpike** (a toll road) branches off I-75 northwest of

Seven Mile Bridge, Florida Keys

Photo Courtesy of Visit Florida

Orlando and slants southeastward across the state until it ends south of Miami in Florida City. For free road maps phone the tourist office for your destination or contact Visit Florida.

Along highways and major urban thoroughfares, many gas stations stay open 24 hours. Most self-service gas stations do not offer car repair, although many sell standard maintenance items. Gasoline (petrol) is sold by the US gallon (1 gallon = 3.8 liters; smaller than the imperial gallon, which equals 4.54 liters).

Photo Courtesy of Visit Florida

Driving in Florida

PRACTICAL INFORMATION

Car Rental		
Company	🖉**Reservation**	**Website**
Alamo	🖉 800-327-9633	www.alamo.com
Budget	🖉 800-527-0700	www.budget.com
Dollar	🖉 800-800-4000	www.dollar.com
Enterprise	🖉 800-325-8007	www.enterprise.com
Hertz	🖉 800-654-3131	www.hertz.com
National	🖉 800-227-7368	www.nationalcar.com
Thrifty	🖉 800-331-4200	www.thrifty.com

(Toll-free numbers not accessible outside US.)

Rental Cars

Most large rental companies have offices at (or near) major airports and downtown locations. Rentals typically include unlimited mileage. If a vehicle is returned at a different location from where it was rented, drop-off charges may be incurred. Reservations are accepted through a toll-free service with a major credit card. Minimum age for rental is 21. A surcharge (*min. $25/ day*) for persons up to age 24 is applied to all rentals in Florida. Be sure to check for proper insurance coverage, offered at extra charge. Liability is not automatically included in the terms of the lease. Drivers are required to have personal-injury protection and property liability insurance; carry proof of insurance in the vehicle at all times.

Recreational Vehicle (RV) Rentals

Motor-home rentals are offered from several locations in Florida. Some models accommodate up to eight people, and service can include free mileage and airport transfers. Make reservations 2–3 weeks in advance. In the summer months (Jun–Aug) and during holiday seasons, reservations should be made at least 4–6 weeks in advance.
Contact Cruise America RV Rentals: *480-464-7300 or 800-671-8042; www.cruiseamerica.com.*

Rules of the Road

The maximum speed limit on interstate highways is 70mph, 60mph on state highways, unless otherwise posted.
Speed limits are generally 30mph within city limits and residential areas. Distances are posted in miles (1 mile=1.6 kilometers). Apart from local authorities, motor clubs (membership required) offer roadside assistance: **American Automobile Association (AAA)** *(800-222-4357; www.aaa.com);* **Shell Motorist Club** *(800-355-7263).*

+ Drive on the **right side** of the road.
+ **Headlights** must be turned on when driving in fog and rain.
+ Foreign visitors bearing **valid driver's licenses** issued by their country of residence

are not required to obtain an International Driver's License in the US.

- **Seat belts** must be worn by all front-seat occupants.
- **Right turns** at a red light are allowed after coming to a complete stop, unless otherwise indicated.
- **Children under 6** must ride in an approved child-safety seats (offered by most car-rental agencies; request these when making reservations).
- Motorists in both directions must come to a complete stop when **warning signals** on a school bus are activated.
- Do not drink and drive.

In Case of Accident

If you are involved in an accident resulting in personal injury or property damage, you must notify the local police and remain at the scene until dismissed.

If blocking traffic, vehicles should be moved as soon as possible. In the case of property damage to an unattended vehicle, the driver must attempt to locate the owner or leave written notice in a conspicuous place of the driver's name, address and car registration number. If you carry a cell phone, **dial FHP (*347)** for the **Florida Highway Patrol**.

By Bus

Florida's largest cities all offer decent local bus services: it's usually inexpensive, and fairly easy to use. In some cities, like Orlando, the local bus line services hotel zones and major attractions, making the bus a real plus if you're visiting the theme parks and don't want to pay for parking.

ACCESSIBILITY
Disabled Travelers

Many of the sights described in this guide are accessible to people with special needs. US Federal law requires that businesses, including hotels and restaurants, provide access for disabled people, devices for people who are hearing impaired, and designated parking spaces. Many public buses are equipped with wheelchair lifts and many hotels have rooms designed for disabled guests.

For more information, contact the **Society for the Advancement of Travel and Hospitality (SATH)**, 347 Fifth Ave., Suite 610, New York, NY 10016 *(212-447-7284; www.sath.org)*.

All **national parks** have facilities for disabled visitors. Free or discounted passes are available. For details, contact the **National Park Service** *(202-208-4747; www.nps.gov/pub_aff/access)*. For **state parks**, check with the **Florida Dept. of Environmental Protection**, Division of Recreation & Parks *(850-245-2157; www. floridastateparks.org/accessforall)*. Passengers who will need assistance with train or bus travel should give advance notice to **Amtrak** *(800-872-7245 or 800-523-6590 (TDD); www.amtrak.com)* or **Greyhound** *(800-752-4841(US only) or 800-345-3109 (TDD); www.greyhound.com)*.

BASIC INFORMATION
Accommodations

Although Florida is a year-round destination, rates are lower **off-season** (May–Oct in South Florida; Dec–Feb in the Panhandle and northern coastal areas). In some hotels, children under 18 stay

PRACTICAL INFORMATION

free when sharing a room with their parents. Some small hotel and many motel rooms include efficiency kitchens, and all but the most basic accommodations are air-conditioned. Hotel taxes, which vary according to location, range from 6% to 12.5%, and are not included in quoted rates.

The **Official Florida Vacation Guide** lists members of the Florida Hotel & Motel Association and is available from **Visit Florida** *(850-488-5607; www.visitflorida.com).* *For a list of suggested lodgings and more information about hotel rates and reservations, see Hotels.*

Hotel Reservations

Rack rates (published rates) provided by hotels are usually higher than website deals. For more information, check with the local convention and visitors bureaus in the area you are visiting, or call the **state-wide hotel information service**: *850-488-5607; www.visitflorida.com.*

Hostels and Campsites

If you're traveling on a tight budget, consider staying at a hostel (*www.hostels.com*) or a campground. Dormitory-style **hostel** rooms average around

$15–$40/night. Private rooms are available at additional charge, and amenities may include swimming pools, air-conditioning, a common living room, laundry facilities, self-service kitchen, dining room and Wi-Fi. Blankets and pillows are provided; linens can be rented.

Campsites are located in national parks, state parks, national forests, along beaches and in private campgrounds. Many campsites are located in central Florida near theme parks: most offer full utility hookups, lodges or cabins and recreational facilities. For a free brochure listing all state park facilities, contact: **Florida Department of Environmental Protection** – Division of Recreation & Parks *(850-245-2157; www. floridastateparks.org).*

KOA Kampgrounds – *(888-562-0000; www.koa.com)* are located all across Florida; some resort properties offer pools, hot tubs, air-conditioned cabins, restaurants, boat ramps, deep-sea fishing and snorkeling.

Discounts

Students, children and senior citizens often get discounts at attractions and hotels. Many establishments offer discounts to persons over age 62, including members of the **American Association of Retired Persons (AARP)** – *(601 E St. N.W., Washington, DC 20049; 888-687-2277; www.aarp.org).*

Business Hours
Banks

Banks are generally open *Mon–Thu 9am–4:30pm, and Fri until 5pm or 6pm*. Some banks in larger cities may be open Saturday morning

Camping, Myakka River State Park

Photo Courtesy of Visit Florida

until noon. Most state and federal government buildings (including city halls) are *open Mon–Fri 8:30am–4:30pm*. Most banks and government offices are closed on major holidays.

Attractions
Hours for individual attractions are given in the text. Closing dates vary; note that most sights and attractions are closed Thanksgiving Day and Dec 25, and many are closed on major holidays (when government offices are closed).

Shops
As a rule, malls and shopping centers are open *Mon–Sat 10am– 9pm, and Sun noon–6pm.*

Pharmacies
Pharmacies are generally open *Mon–Fri 8am–10pm, Sat 9am– 9pm, and Sun 10am–6pm*. Many CVS and Walgreens pharmacies are open 24 hours. Check the Yellow Pages phone directory under "Pharmacies," or ask at your hotel.

Electricity
Electrical current in the US is 120 volts AC, 60 Hz. Foreign-made appliances may need voltage transformers and North American flat-blade adapter plugs (available at specialty travel and electronics stores).

Internet
The Internet is widely available in hotels, Wi-Fi hot spots and at a large number of internet cafes throughout Florida.

Liquor Laws
The legal minimum age for purchase and consumption of

alcoholic beverages is 21; proof of age is required. Most restaurants and bars do not serve liquor prior to 1pm on Sunday. Liquor is sold in liquor stores only, while beer and wine is available at grocery stores. Consuming liquor in public places and carrying an open liquor container in a moving vehicle is illegal.

Mail
Letters can be mailed from most hotels as well as from post offices. Stamps and packing material may be purchased at post offices, grocery stores and businesses offering postal and express-shipping services located throughout the state (*see the Yellow Pages phone directory under "Mailing Services"*). Most post offices are open *Monday–Friday 9am–5pm*, some are also open Saturday 9am–noon.

Money/Currency
Currency is the US Dollar and comes in notes of $1, $5, $10, $20, $50 and $100. Coins come in denominations of 1,5,10, and 25 cents, as well as one dollar.

Banks
Most banks are members of the network of Automated Teller Machines (ATM), allowing visitors from around the world to withdraw cash using bank cards and major credit cards. ATMs can usually be found in airports, banks, grocery stores, shopping malls, and theme parks.

Credit Cards
All major credit cards are accepted in hotels, most restaurants, stores, entertainment venues and gas

Clinton Square Market, Key West

© Richard Nowitz/Apa Publications

stations in Florida. To report a lost or stolen credit card:

American Express – 800-528-4800
Diners Club Card – 800-234-6377
Master Card – 800-627-8372
Visa – 800-947-2911

Traveler's Checks

Most banks will cash brand-name traveler's checks and process cash advances on major credit cards with proper identification. Traveler's checks are accepted at most stores, restaurants and hotels. **American Express Co. Travel Service** *(www.americanexpress.com)* has offices in Jacksonville, Miami and other major Florida cities.

Currency Exchange

Currency can be exchanged at most banks (fee applies). Currency-exchange services are also available at the major international airports in Jacksonville, Miami, Orlando and Tampa. **Thomas Cook Currency Services** operates exchange offices throughout Florida *(800-287-7362; www.thomascook.com)*.

Smoking

Smoking is banned in most enclosed indoor workplaces and public spaces, including restaurants. Exceptions include stand-alone bars, where food is merely incidental, and tobacco shops.

Taxes and Tips

Prices displayed or quoted in the US do not generally include **sales tax** (6% in Florida). Sales tax is added at the time of purchase and is not reimbursable (it can sometimes be avoided if purchased items are shipped to another country by the seller). The hotel occupancy tax (6%–12.5%) and tax rate for rental cars vary according to location; daily surcharges may be added as well. Some counties levy an additional local sales tax, and/or a 1%–5% tourist tax.

Tipping – In the US it is customary to give a tip for services rendered by waiters/waitresses, porters, hotel maids and taxi drivers. In restaurants, patrons normally tip the server 15%–20% of the bill. (In popular tourist locations restaurants may automatically add a service charge; check your bill before you leave a tip). At hotels, porters are generally given $1 per suitcase, housekeeping staff $1 per day. Taxi drivers are usually tipped 15% of the fare.

Telephones

Some public telephones accept credit cards, and all will accept long-distance calling cards. For **long-distance calls** in the US and Canada, dial 1 + area code (3 digits) + number (7 digits). To place a **local call**, dial the 7-digit number without 1 or the area code (unless the local calling area includes several area codes).

To find a **long-distance** number, dial 1 + area code + 555-1212 (*there is a charge for both services*). For

Important Phone Numbers	
Emergencies (police, fire department)	🕿**911**
Directory Assistance	🕿411

operator assistance or information, dial **0** for the local operator or **00** for the long-distance operator. To place an **international call**, dial **011** + country code + area code + number. A list of country and city codes can be found in the beginning of local phone directories. To place a collect call (person receiving the call pays charges), dial **0** + area code + number and tell the operator you are calling collect. If it is an international call, ask for the overseas operator.

Most telephone numbers in this guide that start with **800** or **888** or **877** are toll free (no charge) in the US and may not be accessible outside North America. Dial 1 before dialing a toll-free number. Most hotels add a surcharge for both local and long-distance calls.

Temperature and Measurement

In the US temperatures are measured in degrees Fahrenheit and measurements are expressed

Hurricane Safety Tips

Hurricanes begin as tropical depressions and are classified as hurricanes once winds reach a speed of 74mph. Never take a hurricane lightly. When staying in coastal areas, be sure to familiarize yourself with evacuation routes, and follow instructions issued by the local authorities.

according to the US Customary System of weights and measures.

Time Zone

Most of Florida is on Eastern Standard Time (EST), 5 hours behind Greenwich Mean Time (GMT). The Panhandle region west of the Apalachicola River adheres to Central Standard Time (CST), 1 hour behind EST.
Daylight Saving Time (clocks are advanced 1hr) is in effect for most of the US from the second Sunday in March until the first Sunday in November.

Castillo de San Marcos, St. Augustine

THE SUNSHINE STATE

Ask ten people what they picture when they hear the word Florida, and you're liable to get ten different answers. Many will think of beaches and palm trees; others, swamps and alligators. Some will picture hordes of senior citizens; others, packs of college kids on spring break. Some will have visions of the Cinderella Castle at Walt Disney World, others the Castillo de San Marcos, the massive stone fort that has been guarding St. Augustine since the early 18C. Or the posh Breakers resort in Palm Beach. Or the swanky Art Deco Delano hotel in Miami Beach.

And the thing is, they would all be right. Of all the United States, Florida ranks among the most complex. This is due in no small part to its long, complex history, traces of which are still evident throughout the state.

PREHISTORIC FLORIDA TO THE FIRST SPANISH PERIOD –

Prehistoric peoples probably inhabited parts of what is now Florida as early as 10,000 BC, and the first semi-permanent settlements began to spring up along Florida's waterways around 5,000 BC. By the time Europeans came ashore in the early 16C, Florida natives numbered around 100,000 but were soon virtually wiped out by the war and disease brought by the colonists.

While others certainly saw Florida from the sea, Spanish explorer **Juan Ponce de León** made the first recorded – and officially sanctioned – landfall, in 1513. De León gave the name La Florida ("flowery") to an area that covers most of the present-day Southeast, west to the Mississippi River and north into the Carolinas. Following Florida's "discovery," Spain made repeated forays to the region to find gold and set up a working colony but met with disastrous results. Storms, hunger and illness ravaged all the expeditions, leading the country to lose interest in the area until 1565, when Spain sent Pedro Menéndez de Avilés to crush a French Huguenot settlement that had taken root near the mouth of the St. Johns River and to establish **St. Augustine**, the first permanent European settlement in Florida and still its most charming historical town. Five years later, the first **citrus** plants were brought here from the Caribbean, starting an industry that still thrives today, with Florida providing nearly half the world's supply of orange juice. Although Spain retained her power in Florida for the next two centuries, the region attracted few independent settlers outside the military and the Catholic

Florida Fast Facts
Nickname: The Sunshine State
State flower: Orange blossom
Total population: 18,801,310
Most populous city: Jacksonville
Capital: Tallahassee
Number of annual visitors: 81 million
Area: 58,560 square miles
Length of shoreline: 1,200 miles

Florida Oranges

Photo Courtesy of Visit Florida

Church. Besides two garrisons at Pensacola and St. Augustine, the Spanish presence consisted of about 100 **missions**, designed to convert and centralize – and thus control – the Indians, who were coerced into labor and defense of the Spanish frontier. Ultimately the system failed. By the early years of the 18C, most missions had been burned in raids by British soldiers and Indians, and the remaining structures, made of palm thatch and wood, quickly deteriorated.

BRITISH RULE AND THE SECOND SPANISH PERIOD

Under the 1763 **Treaty of Paris** ending the Seven Years War between England and France, the Spanish colony was ceded to Britain in exchange for Havana, Cuba, which England had captured the previous year. In contrast to Spain, Britain built a self-supporting colony, establishing sugar, rice, indigo and cotton plantations along the St. Johns River. At the same time, a number of loosely organized Indian groups (later known as the Creek Confederacy) had begun to filter into northern Florida, pushed by

settlers out of Georgia, Alabama and South Carolina. From the Creeks, two main nations, the Hitchiti-speaking **Miccosukee** and the Muskogee-speaking **Seminoles**, emerged.

British occupation of Florida was to last only 20 years. With Britain's forces engaged in Revolutionary War battles farther north, Spain took the opportunity to recapture Pensacola in 1781, and under the **Second Treaty of Paris** (1783) ending the Revolution, Florida reverted to Spanish control. But this period was short-lived as well. During the War of 1812, violence erupted repeatedly between white settlers and Indians, and from 1817 to 1818 General Andrew Jackson led the first of a series of raids against the Seminoles (the **First Seminole War**) and the Spanish. Unable to maintain control of this unruly territory, Spain handed over Florida to the US in 1821.

THE BIRTH OF MODERN FLORIDA

Even more than other tribes, the Seminoles fiercely resisted US government efforts to move them to reservations in the west, resulting in two more

T.T. Wentworth, Jr. Florida State Museum

devastating **Seminole wars** between 1835 and 1858. Amid all this turbulence, Florida was admitted to the Union as the **27th state** in 1845. During early statehood, settlement centered around Tallahassee. Hundreds of **plantations** flourished by 1850, building a cotton economy comparable to that of antebellum Georgia. To protect its slave-based economy, Florida seceded from the Union in 1861. While the war almost bankrupted the state, Reconstruction brought new investors from the north, ready to finance business, land speculation, transportation and – most important – **tourism**.

Railroad tycoons **Henry Bradley Plant** and **Henry Morrison Flagler** arrived in the state in the late 19C, linking the west and east coasts, respectively, to the north and opening the way to large-scale beachfront development. Extravagant hotels, like the still luxurious Breakers of Palm Beach, were strategically placed at each new railhead, drawing the cream of the northern social set in the late 19C. The good times continued into the early 20C, Florida's gilded age. Millionaire industrialists luxuriated in fabulous villas, while movie stars arrived from Hollywood to make films in **Jacksonville**, then a leading motion-picture production center. With the advent of good roads and the affordable Model T automobile, the middle class began making its way to Florida as well. From 1920 to 1925, the state grew four times as fast as any other, with real estate prices spiraling upward accordingly. The bubble burst in 1926, its devastation augmented by the Great Depression in 1929. After several decades of slow growth, Florida tourism rebounded in the postwar years. More new hotels appeared in Greater Miami between 1945 and 1954 than in all the other US states combined. In 1958 the first US domestic jet service, from New York to Miami, opened the way for more tourists. Highway travel increased, too, and with it small attractions – featuring everything from alligators to mermaids – mushroomed along the Florida roadside.

These private businesses were the forerunners of **Walt Disney World**, which opened in Orlando to great fanfare in 1971, soon becoming one of the top tourist attractions in the world.

FLORIDA TODAY

A majority of Florida's tourists – 50 million out of a total of 80 million – still flock to the Orlando area to frolic at its three over-the-top commercial theme parks (**SeaWorld** and **Universal Studios** joined Disney in 1973 and 1990). But for those who wish to venture farther afield, Florida has much to offer. Despite the 2008 real estate crash, cities all over Florida are adding new attractions and

Florida's Gentle Giant

Florida's official marine mammal, the **manatee** is closely related to the elephant. Full-grown manatees can live up to 60 years, measure up to 13ft long, and weigh more than 3,000 pounds. Indeed, these herbivorous creatures can pack away up to 100 pounds of aquatic vegetation per day, earning them the nickname "sea cows." Manatees have no natural enemies except humans: development of the state's coastal areas has diminished their feeding grounds, forcing the slow-moving mammals into boating areas where they often become injured or killed in collisions.

In 1973 manatees were listed as an endangered species, and in 1978 the whole of Florida became a manatee sanctuary. As of January 2011, there may be fewer than 5,000 of these gentle giants in Florida waters. By contrast, once-endangered alligators now number over a million.

revamping old ones. With just a few years under its belt, the annual **Miami International Art Fair** has established itself as one of the hottest in the world, and the sizzling city itself continues to attract top-tier restaurateurs and hoteliers. And once-sleepy St. Petersburg is revamping its waterfront with the help of the spectacular new **Dalí Museum**. Inland, an effort to restore more natural water flow to the world-famous **Everglades** – American's "river of grass" – is reviving habitat for more than 60 threatened and endangered species there, as well as improving the health of the 150mi-long arc of **coral reefs** that fringe Florida's famous **Keys**. Indeed, this sleepy string of islands, culminating in the laid-back playground of **Key West**, could not feel more remote from the glitz of Miami or the commercial frenzy of Orlando. And that is exactly what is so wonderful about Florida. In a single day you could, theoretically, ride a bone-rattling roller coaster, tour a world-class art museum, sunbathe on one of the country's finest beaches, kayak through a cypress swamp, and fly on a zip-wire over an alligator habitat. But then what would you say when asked which of those things represented the "real" Florida? "All of the above"?

Relaxing in Key West

THE SUNSHINE STATE

EVERGLADES

Renowned throughout the world, the vast "river of grass" known as the **Everglades★★★** covers the southern end of the Florida peninsula in a subtropical wetland teeming with rare birds, mammals and reptiles. The third-largest national park in the continental US, the 1.5-million-acre preserve is a nature-lover's paradise, offering ample opportunities to cycle, hike, bird-watch, canoe and cruise.

The 50mi-wide sheet of moving water stretching from Lake Okeechobee to the Florida Bay began to form during the last Ice Age, when a shallow tropical sea intermittently covered the area. Averaging 6in in depth and losing only 2in of elevation for every mile it slopes down toward the Gulf of Mexico, the slow-moving river gives rise to diverse and delicate ecosystems: coastal and sawgrass prairies, mangrove swamps, tree islands, pinelands, hardwood hammocks and coastal estuaries. Ideally these are nourished by heavy rains during the wet season (May–Oct) and become parched during the dry winter months, but the complex rhythms of the Glades have been interrupted in the past century by the human manipulation of water flow and encroaching development. Grassroots pressure over the years to protect the Everglades is finally bearing fruit, and the area is gradually returning to its natural state, with laws in effect to limit pollutants from nearby cities and farms, remove invasive foreign plants, and dismantle infrastructure that impedes the river's flow. The first phase of one such project, the replacement of the Tamiami Trail highway (US-41) with a series of bridges, is on schedule for completion in 2013.

View of Ten Thousand Islands

© ARCO/G. Schulz/age fotostock

Touring Tip

While a visit to the Everglades is an easy day-trip from Miami, we recommend three days to get a good sense of this unique environment. In the north, be sure to take the **Shark Valley Tram Tour★**, go on a **cruise of the Ten Thousand Islands★★**, and hike through the eerily beautiful forest at **Big Cypress Bend★★•** in Fakahatchee Strand Preserve. The southern section, organized as a driving tour below, offers abundant alligator-viewing on the **Anhinga Trail★★**, guided canoe trips, and an astounding **overlook★★** at Pa-hay-okee ("grassy waters," in the language of the Calusa Indians).

Practical Information

The Everglades is a largely wild, swamp-like environment, so be sure to plan accordingly. Always carry water, sunscreen, and insect repellent with you, and tell someone of your itinerary if you plan to hike or paddle alone. No pets are allowed on trails. Smoking is likewise prohibited. While wildlife viewing is one of the highlights of a visit (bring binoculars), do not disturb or feed animals. Backcountry camping permits are required for all overnight trips and may be obtained at visitor centers.

When to Go

The best time to visit is definitely in **winter** during the dry season (Nov–mid-Apr), when daytime temperatures range from 60° to 80°F, mosquitoes are tolerable, and wildlife is easier to spot. Most ranger-led walks and talks are limited to this period as well. The busiest week is Dec 25–Jan 1, so make lodging and tour reservations several months in advance. In **summer** (May–Oct) the Park is, unsurprisingly, less crowded (by humans at least) as temperatures often soar to 95°F and the hot, humid weather brings clouds of mosquitoes and other biting insects.

Getting There

♦ **By Air - Miami International Airport (MIA)** — 34mi north of Homestead, is the closest commercial airport (*305-876-7000; www.miami-airport.com*). Major rental-car agencies are located at the airport.

♦ **By Car -** There are two main entrances to **Everglades National Park**. The **Ernest F. Coe Visitor Center** (*open year-round daily 8am–5pm*), 11mi southwest of Homestead on Rte. 9336, flanks the southern entrance. The **Shark Valley** visitor center (*open year-round daily 8:30am–5:15pm*) is on US-41 (Tamiami Trail), 30mi west of Miami. The entrance fee is $10/vehicle, valid at both park entrances for 7 days.

Visitor Information

Park Headquarters is located at 40001 State Rd. 9336, in Homestead (*305-242-7700; www.nps.gov/ever*). In addition to the visitor centers at the main entrances listed above, there are several centers located throughout the park at key sites, including **Everglades City**, the embarkation point for cruises of the Ten Thousand Islands, and **Flamingo**, the terminus of the southern route. **Fakahatchee Strand Preserve State Park** and **Big Cypress National Preserve** also have their own visitor centers.

A Haven for Wildlife

One of the major wetlands left on the North American continent, the Everglades supports some 600 species of animals, including 350 types of birds, 60 species of mosquitoes and 26 kinds of snakes, some of which are found nowhere else in the world. The southern Everglades is, in fact, the only place in the world where you'll find both alligators and crocodiles. Crocodiles are far rarer than alligators and may be distinguished by their lighter gray-green coloring (alligators are black), long pointed snout, and lower incisors that protrude from either side of their jaw when their mouth is closed. Birds provide the greatest spectacle in the park, with herons, egrets, ibis, cranes and other waterbirds almost always within sight. Bald eagles and ospreys nest here, and white pelicans – the largest birds on the continent, with a wingspan of 9ft – bed down here for the winter.

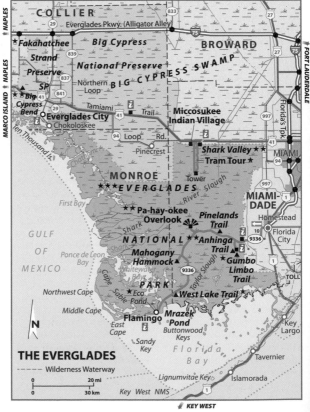

THE EVERGLADES

- - - - Wilderness Waterway

SOUTHERN EVERGLADES

A solitary highway cuts through the southern section of **Everglades National Park★★★**. Accordingly, sights here are organized as a driving tour from Coe Visitor Center in the northeast to Flamingo in the south. But be sure to get out of the car—a series of trails and visitor centers en route will acquaint you with the quintessential Glades.

🚗 DRIVING TOUR★★

76mi round-trip within park.

Ernest F. Coe Visitor Center

▷ *On Rte. 9336 just before the park entrance.*

Exhibits and films at this attractive facility address the Everglades as well as the environmental crises confronting South Florida generally. Be sure to pick up a park newspaper and inquire about activities going on in the park during your visit.

▷ *Continue 2mi on Rte. 9336 and turn left at the sign for Royal Palm Visitor Center and the Gumbo Limbo and Anhinga trails.*

Anhinga Trail★★
0.5mi.

A popular trail beginning at the back of the Royal Palm Visitor Center, it begins as a wide paved path and continues as a boardwalk leading across Taylor Slough, a shallow, slow-moving river that tunnels through a marsh dense with willow thickets and palm trees. Alligators, turtles and myriad birds congregate here, particularly in the winter months.

Gumbo Limbo Trail★
0.4mi.

This trail weaves through the luxuriant vegetation of **Paradise Key Hammock**, the area that formed the first protected piece of

Anhinga , Everglades National Park
© Michael Braun Photography/iStockphoto.com

the Everglades, **Royal Palm State Park**, established in 1916. A typical tropical island of hardwood trees, Paradise Key supports a rich variety of ferns, lianas, orchids, royal palms, and, of course, gumbo-limbo trees. The latter are known in Florida as "tourist trees" because their red, peeling bark resembles the sunburned skin of visitors who lingered too long on the beach.

▷ *Return to Rte. 9336 and continue 4.4mi.*

Pinelands Trail
0.5mi.

A paved trail here circles through a rocky, drier landscape that supports one of the few existing forests of **Florida slash pine**. Excessive logging in the early 20C, along with the suppression of forest fires that allow pine to compete with hardwoods, has led to the demise of the pine forests that once covered much of southern Florida.

Only 20,000 acres of slash pine remain, making this species the continent's most endangered member of the pine family.

○ *Continue 6.3mi to the turn-off for Pa-hay-okee Overlook.*

Pa-hay-okee Overlook★★

This elevated platform provides a sweeping **view★★** of the Everglades' seemingly endless sawgrass prairie. Part of the sedge family, sawgrass is by far the most dominant flora in the Everglades. As its name implies, its long blades are sharp, but its roots are soft and edible.

○ *Return to Rte. 9336 and drive 7mi; turn right at sign for Mahogany Hammock.*

Mahogany Hammock Trail 0.5mi.

Tunneling through a lush hammock (stand) of royal palm, gumbo-limbo and mahogany trees, this boardwalk trail passes the largest known mahogany tree in the country.

○ *Return to Rte. 9336 and continue 11.3mi; turn right to parking area for West Lake.*

West Lake Trail★ 0.5mi.

Follow the boardwalk here along the edge of West Lake across a mangrove swamp. Three types of mangroves thrive in Florida's coast areas where freshwater and saltwater mix: red, distinguished by their reddish arcing roots; black, whose bases are surrounded by spiky breathing tubes called pneumatophores; and white, generally found on drier ground.

○ *Continue 3.6mi.*

Mrazek Pond

Right by the road, this watering hole is popular with birders. At dawn and dusk, grebes, herons, egrets, ibis and roseate spoonbills congregate here to feast on fish and shellfish.

○ *Continue 3.5 mi to Flamingo.*

Flamingo
Located at the southern terminus of Rte. 9336 (38mi from park entrance).

This small outpost overlooking Florida Bay provides the only food and camping facilities in this part of the park. The **visitor center** *(open Dec–Apr daily 7:30am–5pm; rest of the year daily 9am–5pm; 941-695-2945)* houses a small display area with natural history exhibits.

The adjacent marina *(239-695-3101)* serves as the boarding point for **boat cruises★★** that tour the backcountry canals and the open waters of Florida Bay; you may also rent **canoes** here.

Man-made **Eco Pond★** *(0.9mi west of visitor center)* is a bird-watcher's paradise, particularly at dawn and dusk when flocks of waterfowl and wading birds gather to feed here on fish and shellfish. The observation platform provides an excellent vantage point.

NORTHERN EVERGLADES

Completed in 1928, the Tamiami Trail (US-41) cuts across the Everglades, linking Miami on the east coast with Naples on the west coast and passing through swampland and sawgrass prairie in between. Because most of the region is wilderness, its main attractions are listed in *The Great Outdoors* section.

There are two exceptions. **Miccosukee Indian Village** *(open year-round daily 9am–5pm; $10/includes optional guided tour; 305-223-8380; www.miccosukeetribe.com)*, .5mi west of Shark Valley, is a commercial venture run by a tribe that has inhabited the area since the mid-19C. It includes chickees (palm-thatched huts), beadwork and patchwork demonstrations, a museum, alligator-wrestling shows and airboat rides. **Everglades City**, 4mi south of US-41 on Rte. 29, is the gateway to the northwestern Everglades, with a few motels and restaurants where one can bed down or fuel up for a canoe trip or cruise of the Ten Thousand Islands. Also in town, the **Gulf Coast Visitor Center** *(open year-round daily 7:30am–5pm; 941-695-3311)* provides information on getting out on the water.

Shark Valley★★

See p37 for visitor center hours.

Named for the shallow, slow-flowing slough that empties into the brackish – and shark-infested – Shark River to the southwest, Shark Valley is actually a basin that lies a few feet lower than the rest of the Everglades. Travel the 15mi loop road via bicycle *(rentals available for $7.75/hr)* or **open-air tram★** *(late Dec–Apr hourly, 9am–4pm; May–late Dec 9:30am, 11am, 1pm, 3pm; 305-221-8455; www.shark valleytramtours.com)*. On the tram tour, park naturalists point out

Observation tower, Shark Valley
© Zoran Ivanovich/iStockphoto.com

some of the local denizens: snail kites, egrets, herons, alligators and gar fish, to name a few.

The Rap on Reptiles

The sluggish-looking alligator can sprint at speeds up to 15mph for distances of 50 yards and swim at a speeds up to 16mph. There are six types of poisonous snakes in Florida: the pygmy rattlesnake, eastern diamondback rattlesnake, canebrake rattler, coral snake, Florida cottonmouth (a.k.a. water moccasin), and southern copperhead. The small dark lizards you see everywhere in Florida are Cuban brown anoles, a species introduced into the state from the West Indies. Its lesser-seen relative, the green anole, is a Florida native.

THE GREAT OUTDOORS

While the Southern Everglades are beautiful to look at, exploration is limited to a few short, if rewarding, trails off the main road. By contrast, the Northern Everglades offer abundant opportunities to experience this world-famous environment. All the sights listed below are in the Northern Everglades.

EVERGLADES

MUST DO

Big Cypress Bend★★

This 1mi boardwalk loop trail provides a glimpse of luxuriant **Fakahatchee Strand Preserve State Park**★ *(entrance on US-41 7mi west of Rte. 29; open year-round daily 8am–dusk; 239-695-4593; www.floridastateparks.org)*, leading through eerily beautiful virgin cypress forest and ending at a swamp frequented by alligators. Elsewhere, the park, known as the "Amazon of North America," comprises a 20mi-long swamp forest, between 3 and 5 miles wide, containing a dense, exotic mix of vegetation. Its flora includes the largest stand of native **royal palm** in the US, as well as the greatest

concentration and diversity of **orchids** (31 threatened and endangered species); 15 species of bromeliads; and a variety of epiphytes, or air plants. Big Cypress is also favored by dwindling numbers of the endangered Florida panther. Guided canoe trips are offered; call ahead to reserve a spot.

Wilderness Waterway

A paradise for boaters and canoeists, this watery inland course twists 99mi through protected rivers and bays from Everglades City to Flamingo. Markers designate the waterway, and campsites (some furnished with chickee shelters) punctuate the route, which takes 6–8hrs by motorboat and 8–10 days by canoe. Keep in mind that permits are required for overnight camping; find permits and maps at the ranger stations in **Flamingo** *(239-695-2945)* and **Everglades City** *(239-695-3311)*.

⚓ Cruises of the Ten Thousand Islands★★

Tours depart from the Gulf Coast Ranger Station in Everglades City year-round daily 8:30am–5pm. Round-trip 1hr 30min. Commentary. $26.50. 239-695-2591. evergladesnationalpark boattoursgulfcoast.com.

Big Cypress Bend boardwalk

© Richard Nowitz/Apa Publications

Park-sponsored cruises offer a look at the marine world of **Chokoloskee Bay**. Countless small islets here are covered collectively with one of the largest mangrove forests in the world. During the cruise you may see dolphins, manatees and numerous waterbirds, including ospreys, herons, roseate spoonbills, and perhaps even nesting bald eagles. To get a closer look, take the **mangrove wilderness tour** (*1hr45min; $35/person*), which explores swampy areas of the park on a six-passenger vessel; or rent kayaks and canoes at the ranger station *(single kayaks $45/day; double kayaks $55/day; canoes $24/day)*.

Big Cypress National Preserve

Accessible from I-75 and US-41. Open daily year-round. 239-695-1201. www.nps.gov/bicy.

Contiguous to the northern Everglades, the 729,000-acre preserve protects a portion of the 2,400sq mi Big Cypress Swamp, a rich variegated wetland covered with forests of bald cypress trees. Few giant cypresses still stand, having been heavily logged early in the 20C, and much of the terrain is now covered with dwarf cypress and sawgrass prairie.
But it is still a major habitat for much of the same wildlife found in the Everglades, particularly the endangered Florida panther, about 30–35 of which are thought to live in the park, and black bears. Rangers lead guided hikes and canoe trips in high season (Nov–Apr). The trips are free, but reservations are recommended.

The Florida Panther
Experts believe that only 50 to 70 of these big tawny-brown cats—designated Florida's state animal—still roam the state's wetlands, the only habitat left for them in the eastern US. The panther's birthrate of two to four kittens every other spring has been diminished by infertility caused by mercury-contaminated prey. Secretive and difficult to spot, adults stand about 2 feet high and weigh between 60 and 130 pounds.

There are two visitor centers in the park, both on US-41 (Tamiami Trail): the **Big Cypress Swamp Welcome Center** *(5mi east of Rte. 29; 239-695-4758)* and the **Oasis Visitor Center** *(19 mi west of Shark Valley; 239-695-1201)*; both have exhibits on flora and fauna and are open year-round daily 9am–4:30pm.
Stroll along the boardwalks near both centers to enjoy views of the swamps and their resident alligators.
Behind the Oasis Visitor Center, the **Florida National Scenic Trail** leads 21mi into the heart of the preserve. A 26mi loop road (*Rte. 94 from Forty Mile Bend to Monroe Station*) circles through haunting cypress swamps in the southern part of the preserve—look for alligators, soft-shell turtles and raptors on the way.
An unpaved northern loop (*16.5mi*) begins at Route 839 and travels through wide-open sawgrass prairie *(follow Turner River Rd./Rte. 839 north 7.3mi; turn left on Rte. 837 to Birdon Rd./Rte. 841, which leads back to US-41)*.

FLORIDA KEYS

Curving southwest 220mi from Biscayne Bay to the Dry Tortugas, the thousand-some islands and islets that compose the Florida Keys form a narrow archipelago separating the waters of the Atlantic from Florida Bay and, farther south, the Gulf of Mexico. With the exception of the northernmost sand islands, the Keys consist of the remains of coral reefs that began forming as early as 10 to 15 million years ago, when the area was covered by a shallow sea. In the early days of settlement, the only means of transportation between the islands was by boat. Today, some islands are still reachable only by boat, while most are linked together by the southernmost stretch of US-1, constructed along the path of Henry Flagler's Overseas Railroad (1912–1935).

The Upper and Middle Keys serve as a jumping-off point for sportfishermen, divers, snorkelers and wildlife enthusiasts interested in the wealth of marine life on the largest living **coral reef** in North America. A boat trip is highly recommended, but abundant state parks and nature areas offer ample opportunities to learn about the reef and its inhabitants, including dolphins, without leaving land. Though beaches are common to most parts of South Florida, they are surprisingly few and far between here – the reef blocks waves from bringing large quantities of sand inland.

Composed of 288 135ft sections soaring some 65ft over the Atlantic, the **Seven-Mile Bridge★★** links the Middle and Lower Keys and offers breathtaking views of the open ocean. The Lower Keys are dominated by the **funky, historic town of Key West★★★**, onetime home of the charismatic author **Ernest Hemingway**.

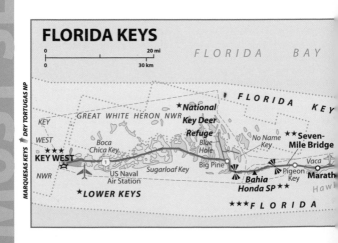

Practical Information

When to Go

December through April is considered high season in the Keys; afternoon temperatures range from 73°F to 79°F. Rainfall is considerably less in the Keys than on the mainland and is usually limited to brief thunderstorms on summer afternoons. March is the pinnacle of Spring Break, when hordes of young people descend on the Keys and Key West. The Florida Keys Tourism Council *(www.fla-keys.com; 800-FLA-KEYS)* **offers information on all aspects of visiting the Keys, including a free smart-phone app.**

Getting There and Around

◆ **By Air** - **Key West International Airport** *(305-296-5439; www.key westinternationalairport.com)* is serviced by most domestic airlines. Rental-car agencies are located at and near the airport. International flights connect through Miami International Airport.

◆ **By Boat** - Key West Express operates **ferries** between Key West and Fort Myers year-round *(3.5hrs; $146 round-trip; 888-539-2628; www.seakeywest.com)*.

◆ **By Car** - Small green **mile-marker (MM) posts** along US-1 give the distance of any given location from Key West; much of the route is two-lane.

The best places along US-1 to find lodging, restaurants and amenities are **Key Largo** (MM 110–87), **Islamorada** (MM 86–66), **Marathon** (MM 65–40), **Big Pine Key** (MM 39–9) and **Key West** (MM 0).

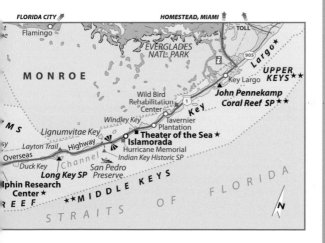

FLORIDA KEYS

ISLANDS

Upper and Middle Keys★★

The **Upper Keys**, the northern-most islands in the group, stretch from **Key Largo★** to Long Key. The first and largest of the keys, Key Largo (pop. 11,000) is 26mi long but at most only 1mi wide; culturally it's still best known for the eponymous 1948 Humphrey Bogart film (almost entirely shot in Hollywood). Proclaiming itself the Dive Capital of the World, Key Largo indeed has many superb dive sites as well as the dazzling **John Pennekamp Coral Reef State Park★★** (see Great Outdoors). **Islamorada** comprises six islands—Plantation Key, Windley Key, Upper Matecumbe Key, Lower Matecumbe Key, Indian Key and Lignumvitae Key—and is known as the Sport Fishing Capital of the World (sportfishing information: 888-FISH-KEYS). Farther south, **Long Key State Park** (305-664-4815; www.floridastateparks.org) offers paddling (kayak rentals), snorkeling, fishing and camping, as well as tropical nature trails. The **Middle Keys** extend from Conch Key to the end of the **Seven Mile Bridge★★**, the longest segmental bridge in the world. **Marathon**, a 10-mile-long family-oriented fishing community located mainly on Vaca, Fat Deer and Grassy Key, is the largest settlement here. All along the route—but especially on the bridge—US-1 offers sweeping views of the blue Atlantic. Be sure to stop by the **Dolphin Research Center★** and the **Crane Point Museums and Nature Point★** for a closer look at the flora and fauna of the Keys (See Animal Parks and Museums).

Lower Keys★

Scrub and slash pine characterize this handful of wooded islands extending from Mile Marker 45 to the outskirts of Key West at MM 5. The low, wet land and surrounding waters provide refuge for a variety of wildlife, including the great white heron and the diminutive Key deer. The latter are found in abundance at **National Key Deer Refuge★** on Big Pine Key, while **Bahia Honda**

Preserving the Reef

The coral reef that lies off Key Largo forms part of the **Florida Reef★★★**, the largest living coral reef system in North America and third-largest barrier reef in the world (after Australia's Great Barrier Reef and the Belize Barrier Reef). Descending to depths of nearly 80ft, it consists of calcium carbonate (limestone) secreted over thousands of years by colonies of small, soft-bodied coral polyps, and protects nearly 200mi of coastline.

Coral requires water of a certain salinity, temperature and clarity to thrive, but over the years, these factors have been thrown out of balance by pollution, overharvesting and careless use. A comprehensive management plan and water-quality protection program developed for the **Florida Keys National Marine Sanctuary** is attempting to reverse the destructive trend and restore this national treasure to full health.

MUST SEE FLORIDA KEYS

Tightrope juggler, Mallory Square Dock

State Park★★ boasts one of the few sand beaches in the Keys (*see Great Outdoors*). Divers flock to the unusually clear waters of the reef at **Looe Key**, part of the Florida Keys National Marine Sanctuary *(information: 305-872-2215 or 877-816-3483; www.diveflakeys.com)*.

Key West★★★

Pirates, wreckers, writers, US presidents and Cuban freedom fighters have all found a haven on this small island at the southernmost tip of the continent. Closer to Havana than Miami, Key West (pop. 25,031) cultivates an atmosphere of sublime laissez-faire that encourages an eclectic mix of residents, from old-time "conch" families (descended from the island's original settlers) to a more recently arrived gay community. The 200-square-block area of the **Old Town★★** ranks as one of the largest National Historic Districts in the US, with more than 3,000 significant structures, many of them quirky, pastel-painted Victorians. Aside from strolling the picturesque streets, there is much

to see and do in town. **Duval Street**, the overtly commercial main stem, bustles with restaurants, bars and boutiques along its north end. **Mallory Square** harbors souvenir vendors, craft shops and eateries, and its adjacent dock provides a berth for the large cruise ships that call at Key West.

Come to **Mallory Square Dock** for the 🌅 **sunset celebration★★** to watch street performers, jugglers, clowns, musicians, and artists strut their stuff in a blaze of golden light.

Getting Oriented in Key West

A good place to start your visit is the **Key West Chamber of Commerce Visitor Center** *(510 Greene St at Duval; open year-round Mon–Fri 8am–6:30pm, weekends 9am–6pm; 305-294-2587 or 800-527-8539; www.key westchamber.org)*, where you can find out about special events and tours (walking and trolley) and pick up brochures on attractions, restaurants and lodging.

MUSEUMS

Crane Point Museums and Nature Point★

MM 50, in Marathon.
Open year-round Mon–Sat 9am–
5pm, Sun noon–5pm. Closed major
holidays. $12.50. 305-743-9100.
www.cranepoint.net.

Trails wind through 63 acres of tropical forest connecting a **Museum, Children's Activities Center, Adderly House** (a Bahamian Conch house built in 1903, made of Bahamian tabby) and **Marathon Wild Bird Center**. Check out the museum for information about local flora and fauna, marine life on the coral reef, and collections of native tree snails and butterflies.

Mel Fisher Maritime Heritage Society★

200 Greene St., Key West. Open
year-round Mon–Fri 8:30am–5pm
& Sat–Sun 9:30am–5pm. $12.50.
305-294-2633. www.melfisher.org.

The don of modern treasure hunters, **Mel Fisher** set up this museum in a former Navy building.

Exhibits here recount the story of the discovery of the *Nuestra Señora de Atocha* and the *Santa Margarita*, two Spanish galleons that sank in the Florida Straits in 1622. Fisher, who died in 1998, is the man behind the salvage. He spent 16 years and lost a son in his unswerving pursuit of the wreck. In 1985 his crew found their prize on the ocean floor; spoils included a 77.76-carat natural emerald crystal and a gold bar weighing over 6 troy pounds. Displays on the first floor feature some of the fabulous gold, silver, gems and other artifacts recovered from the dive site. The second floor is devoted to special exhibits.

Gold and silver treasure, Mel Fisher Maritime Heritage Society

© Richard Nowitz/Apa Publications

Key West at Night

Key West is a town of extremes. It's the southernmost city in the United States, known for its ultimate laid-back island charm. And one of Key West's most eccentric claims to fame is the daily celebration of sunset. Ever wonder why? That means it's time to get the party started! That's what they've been doing at the **Green Parrot Bar** (*601 Whitehead St.; 305-294-6133; www.greenparrot. com*) since the 1920s. The real question, however, is which of two rivals is Ernest Hemingway's authentic hangout? The original **Sloppy Joe's** (*201 Duval St.; 305-294-5717; www.sloppyjoes.com*) moved across the street from its original location in 1937, and although Papa did frequent the new location, the owners of the original site, now called **Captain Tony's** (*428 Greene St.; 305-294-1838; www.capttonyssaloon.com*) still claim bragging rights.

HISTORIC SITES

Ernest Hemingway Home and Museum★★

907 Whitehead St at Olivia, Key West. Open year-round daily 9am–5pm. $12.50. 305-294-1136. www.hemingwayhome.com.

Half-hidden amid lush vegetation, this gracious stucco house is where Key West's legendary resident novelist spent much of his time between 1931 and 1939. Sparsely decorated rooms contain period pieces, some of which belonged to the author. In Hemingway's bedroom, notice the **ceramic cat** made for "Papa" by Pablo Picasso. More than 60 felines live on the property today, some supposedly descended from the author's own pets. Hemingway wrote such classics as *Death in the Afternoon*, *For Whom the Bell Tolls* and *To Have and Have Not* in his carriage-house studio. The large **swimming pool** was the first one built on the island.

Harry S Truman Little White House Museum★★

111 Front St. in Truman Annex, Key West. Entrance near Hilton Hotel at the presidential gates on Whitehead St. Open year-round daily 9am–5pm. $15. 305-294-9911. www.trumanlittlewhite house.com.

This large clapboard house, the favorite retreat of America's 33rd president, **Harry S Truman** (1884–1972), gives a rare glimpse of the private life of the man the press called "an uncommon common man." Built in 1890, the house was occupied by Thomas

Ernest Hemingway Home, Key West

Photo Courtesy of Visit Florida

Edison during World War I while the inventor worked on his depth charge for the Navy. Truman first visited Key West in 1946, on the advice of his physician. Over his next seven years in office, he spent 175 days of "working vacations" at his "Little White House." He ran the country from the desk that still sits in a corner of the living room.

Audubon House and Tropical Gardens★

205 Whitehead St., Key West. Open year-round daily 9:30am–5pm. $12. 305-294-2116 or 877-294-2470. www.audubonhouse.com.

Capt. John Huling Geiger built this gracious Neoclassical house in the 1840s. Its restoration by Key West native Mitchell Wolfson in 1960 sparked the island's preservation movement. Wolfson dedicated the house to America's premiere ornithologist, **John James Audubon**, who visited Key West in 1832 while working on his authoritative volume *Birds of America*. Decorated in 19C period furnishings, the house is notable for its fine collection of 28 original **Audubon engravings** and for its lush tropical garden.

ANIMAL PARKS

Dolphin Research Center★

MM 59, on Grassy Key. Open year-round daily 9am–4:30pm. Closed major holidays. $20. 305-289-1121. www.dolphins.org.

Bottlenose dolphins and California sea lions demonstrate their amazing abilities as trainers and educators narrate. And kids love to run around in the new **splash playground**. The center also offers a dolphin swim and other interactive programs; call or check website for details.

Theater of the Sea★

MM 84.5 on Windley Key. Open year-round daily 9:30am–4pm. $26.95. 305-664-2431. www.theaterofthesea.com.

Open-air pools teeming with sharks, rays, sea turtles and fish inhabit this 17-acre marine park. Dolphins, parrots and sea lions perform regularly in shows that focus on animal behavior and environmental issues. The park also offers swim-with-the-dolphins and snorkeling excursions (*extra fee; reservations required*), and has a private lagoon beach (*open in season*) and a restaurant.

Dolphin Research Center

© Dolphin Research Center

SHOPPING

The lure of the Florida Keys may be sand and sun, but it's not all about the beach. The Key West shopping scene goes far beyond the tourist-souvenir tchotchkes. **Blue** *(718 Caroline St.; 305-292 5172; www.blueislandstore.com)* and the playfully named **Evan and Elle** *(725 Duval St.; 305-295-3530)* offer high-end designer clothing and accessories for the most discerning shopper. Take a bit of the beach back home with a hammock, porch swing or rocker from the **Key West Hammock Company** *(717 Duval St., Suite 2; 305-293-0008; www.keywesthammockcompany.com)*.

Did you know Key West rivaled Cuba for cigar making? **Key West Cigar** *(1117 Duval St.; 305-296-1977; www.keywestcigar.com)* offers a wide variety of distinctive smokes. If fishing is your obsession, visit **The Saltwater Angler** *(243 Front St.; 305-294-3248; www.saltwaterangler.com)* for the finest in conventional, spin and fly fishing gear, tropical clothing and gifts. And if you can't go home without that tchotchke, you'll find it in the quaint **Bahama Village Market** in Key West's historic district, roughly bordered by Whitehead, Fort, Angela and Catherine streets. And keep an eye out for the famous Key West chickens that roam the city.

THE GREAT OUTDOORS

⚓ Bahia Honda State Park★★

Bahia Honda Key, MM 36.8. Open year-round daily 8am–sundown. $8 per vehicle, plus 50¢/person. 305-872-2353. www.floridastate parks.org/bahiahonda.

If you're searching out beaches in the Keys, Bahia Honda boasts one of the largest stretches of sand **beach★★** in the Keys. Named by the Spanish for its "Deep Bay," Bahia Honda's park covers 524 acres and includes a lagoon, mangrove forest and a tropical hardwood hammock. Swimming is popular in the Atlantic Ocean and Florida Bay, and if you want to go farther afield, rent a kayak and explore the waters around the park.

⚓ John Pennekamp Coral Reef State Park★★

MM 102.5, on Key Largo. Open year-round daily 8am–dusk. $8/ vehicle plus 50¢/person. 850-245-2157. www.pennekamppark.com.

Stretching along Key Largo's coastline and reaching 3mi off-shore, America's first **underwater park** was created in 1960. Some 96 percent of it lies beneath the waves, encompassing a dazzling kaleidoscope of vivid coral and sea creatures. Take in the informative displays (including a floor-to-ceiling aquarium) in the **visitor center** (*open year-round daily 9am–5pm*), which provide an excellent introduction to the undersea world offshore. Then, perhaps, take a **snorkeling** tour—though you'll need a good pair of lungs, or scuba gear, to see the iconic **Statue of Christ of the Abyss**, an 8ft 6in, 4,000-pound bronze sculpture that stands in 25 feet of water.

Dry Tortugas National Park★

69mi southwest of Key West. Accessible only by plane or boat. 305-242-7700. www.nps.gov/drto. *See p13.*

National Key Deer Refuge★

MM 30.5, on Big Pine Key. Open year-round daily dawn–dusk. 305-872-2239. www.fws.gov/ nationalkeydeer.

This National Wildlife Refuge, established in 1954, is the place to spot protected Key deer, the smallest of all North American deer at 2ft tall at the shoulder. Two trails within the refuge provide good opportunities for deer sightings, particularly at dawn and dusk, when they come out to feed.

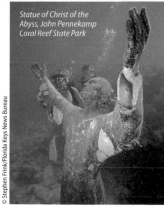

Statue of Christ of the Abyss, John Pennekamp Coral Reef State Park

© Stephen Frink/Florida Keys News Bureau

MIAMI AND SOUTH FLORIDA

Nicknamed the Gold Coast, Florida's most heavily developed strip extends along the Atlantic Ocean in a 70mi-long megalopolis from Miami★★★ to Palm Beach★★★.

There are family-oriented attractions throughout the region, but this is much more of an adult playground than child-friendly Orlando. While the white-sand beaches and clear blue water are big draws, you'll also want to partake of the upmarket shops of Palm Beach's Worth Avenue★★★, the art museums of West Palm Beach, Miami Beach's bright parade of Art Deco architecture, and Miami's cultural melting pot of eateries, nightclubs and festivals. Before the arrival of the first European explorers in the 16C, South Florida was inhabited by Tequesta Indians.

Tourism first came to the area in the 1890s as a result of Henry Flagler's famous Florida East Coast Railway, which began at St. Augustine and finally reached Key West in 1912. Ritzy Palm Beach used to be the crown jewel of the Gold Coast, but in the past couple of decades Miami has transformed itself from a sleazy, even dangerous, metropolis into one of the world's sexiest cities.

Practical Information

When to Go

High season in South Florida is during the **winter** (Oct–Apr). Although the summer months are hot and humid, coastal breezes make them tolerable. Afternoon showers are common from Jun– Sept. The **hurricane season** generally runs from Jun–Nov.

Getting There and Around

◆ **By Air** – The major airports in the region are: **Palm Beach International Airport (PBI)** (*561-471-7420; www.pbia.org*); **Fort Lauderdale–Hollywood International Airport (FLL)** (*866-435-9355; www.broward.org/airport*); and **Miami International Airport (MIA)** (*305-876-7000; www.miami-airport.com*). All have rental-car agencies and connect to public transportation.

◆ **By Train** – **Amtrak** (*800-USA-RAIL; www.amtrak.com*) provides daily service from New York to Miami, stopping at many other Florida stations en route. **Tri-Rail** (*800-TRI-RAIL; www.tri-rail.com*) provides commuter rail service between West Palm Beach and Greater Miami.

◆ **By Car** – Though all South Florida cities have some sort of public bus or light-rail system, it is easiest to get around, and between, cities by car.

Visitor Information

Visitflorida.com has visitor information for the whole state.

SOUTH FLORIDA

0 — 10 mi
0 — 15 km

N. PALM BEACH
John D. MacArthur Beach SP
RIVIERA BEACH
★ WEST PALM BEACH
Lake Worth
PALM BEACH ★★★

★★ Lion Country Safari
ROYAL PALM BEACH
Lake Worth
Lantana

★ Arthur R.
Marshall
Loxahatchee
NWR
Sixmile Bend
Shawano
Visitor Center
★ Morikami Museum
Palm Beach Co.
Broward Co.

BOYNTON BEACH
DELRAY BEACH
Linton Blvd.
Highland Beach
Spanish R. Park
Red Reef Park
BOCA RATON ★
DEERFIELD BEACH

CORAL SPRINGS
Twentysix Mile Bend
Office Depot Center
MARGATE
Tamarac
★ Butterfly World
POMPANO BEACH

PLANTATION
Lauderhill
Flamingo Gardens ▲
PEMBROKE PINES
Miramar
FORT LAUDERDALE ★
Port Everglades
John U. Lloyd Beach SP

Broward Co.
Miami - Dade Co.
OPA-LOCKA
NORTH MIAMI
HOLLYWOOD
Aventura
N. MIAMI BEACH
A1A
Bal Harbour
Surfside
ATLANTIC

★★ MIAMI
★★ Coral Gables
★★ Coconut Grove
KENDALL
S.W. 137th Ave.
S.W. 152nd St.
MIAMI BEACH ★★★
SOUTH BEACH ★★★
Virginia Key Beach Park
Key Biscayne
Bill Baggs Cape Florida SP ★

★★ Zoo Miami
Cutler Ridge

★ Coral Castle
Homestead
Fascell Visitor Ctr.
S.W. 328th St.
★ BISCAYNE NP
Elliott Key
Biscayne Bay
OCEAN

NAPLES ● AH-THA-THI-KI MUSEUM

MIAMI AND SOUTH FLORIDA

53

CITIES

MIAMI★★★

*Art Deco
Architecture
South Beach*

Courtesy of Visit Florida

Renowned for its tantalizing tropical landscape of blue sky, aqua waters and fabulous white beaches, Miami (pop. 391,355) is one of the most popular resort destinations in the US. Each year some ten million visitors from around the world pour into the city and its environs. Aside from the time-honored pastime of sunbathing, there's plenty to do in Miami, from sports such as golf, tennis, yachting, deep-sea fishing, and scuba diving to cultural excursions like gallery hopping, touring historic houses and museums, and clubbing. Because of its key position on the Florida Straits near the southeastern tip of the state, Miami also boasts the world's largest cruise port, accommodating passengers to and from the Caribbean and South America.

The bustling city has a diverse mix of Latinos, Caucasians and African Americans. But it is especially known for its **Cuban** population,

with waves of exiles arriving in the decades following the 1959 Cuban Revolution. Many still hope to return home, provided that Cuba's market economy is restored and their property rights—quashed long ago by Fidel Castro—are honored. Greater Miami embraces all of Miami-Dade County along with numerous islands, including **Miami Beach★★★**, a long, narrow barrier island located 2.5mi off the mainland between Biscayne Bay and the Atlantic Ocean. To the east of downtown lies 7mi-long **Key Biscayne**, home to some of Miami's finest restaurants, hotels and beaches.

MIAMI NEIGHBORHOODS

Downtown

A vibrant 1.5sq mi quarter surrounded on three sides by the warm waters of Biscayne Bay and the Miami River, Miami's downtown exudes the bustling atmosphere of a Latin city. One of its best known landmarks is the **Freedom Tower** *(600 Biscayne Blvd.)*, a Spanish Revival-style pile (1925) whose signature cupola was inspired by the 16C Giralda Tower in Seville, Spain. Thirty-two-acre **Bayfront Park** got a multimillion-dollar facelift in 2009; it sports sculptures, a fountain, a playground and a 6,500-seat amphitheater. At its north end, the hugely popular **Bayside Marketplace★** is an open-air shopping mall with loads of boutiques and eateries. But 29-acre **Museum Park** (formerly Bicentennial Park), seven blocks farther north, is poised to become Miami's new cultural hub, as the **Miami Art Museum** and the **Miami Museum of Science** plan to move into posh new facilities here in 2013 and 2014, respectively

Freedom Tower
© Willey/Dreamstime.com

(see Museums). Nearby, the eye-popping **Arsht Center** is Florida's largest performing arts venue *(see Performing Arts)*.

Little Havana

Immediately east of downtown, the 3.3sq mi section of Miami bounded by the Miami River (east), S.W. 37th Avenue (west), N.W. Seventh Street (north) and Coral Way (south) represents one of the city's liveliest neighborhoods. Along **Calle Ocho**, or Eighth Street – Little Havana's main thoroughfare – sidewalk vendors hawk a variety of wares and ubiquitous stand-up *cafeterias* dispense tiny cups of dense black *café cubano*.

The **Latin Quarter** stretches along Calle Ocho between S.W. 17th and S.W. 12th avenues. Here quaint street lamps rise above brick sidewalks set with stars bearing the names of an international array of prominent Hispanic entertainers, including Julio Iglesias and Gloria Estefan. Cuban history is remembered in places such as **José Martí Park** *(351 S.W. 4th St.)*, named for the apostle of Cuban independence, and the **Cuban Memorial Plaza** *(median of S.W. 13th Ave./Cuban Memorial Blvd. and S.W. 8th St.)*, a hexagonal marble monument erected in honor of those members of Brigade 2506 who lost their lives in the aborted invasion of Cuba in April 1961. **Woodlawn Park Cemetery** *(3260 S.W. 8th St.)*, Miami's largest burial spot, is the final resting place for thousands of Cuban refugees, as well as two former exiled Cuban presidents and Anastasio Somoza, longtime dictator of Nicaragua.

Coral Gables★★

Dubbing itself the "City Beautiful," Coral Gables (www.coralgables.com) covers a 12.5sq mi area just southwest of downtown Miami. While largely residential, this city within a city also boasts the **University of Miami** and some of the area's finest Mediterranean Revival architecture (the **Biltmore Hotel★★**; see Hotels) and tropical landscaping (**Fairchild Tropical Garden★★**; see Great Outdoors). Designed to set Coral Gables apart from surrounding areas, grand drive-through **entrances** built in the 1920s continue to welcome you with suitable pomp, much in the spirit of the triumphal arches of Spanish cities like Seville and Toledo. **Coral Way** is the main east-west artery in downtown Coral Gables. The four-block (half-mile) section between Douglas and LeJeune roads is known as **Miracle Mile** for its mix of shops and restaurants.

Coconut Grove★★

Lush foliage and banyan trees enhance the tropical feeling of this picturesque village stretching 4mi south of Rickenbacker Causeway along Biscayne Bay. The oldest community in the Miami area, Coconut Grove (www.coconutgrove.com) retains a strong sense of history in its quiet residential neighborhoods, where many of the vine-covered bungalows and Mediterranean-style estates date to the early 20C. Its historic heritage includes the 1916 Italian Renaissance-style villa and formal gardens known as **Vizcaya★★★** (see Historic Sites). Centered on the intersection of Grand Avenue and Main Highway, **Coconut Grove Village★** contains a mix of high-end shops and boutiques on **Streets of Mayfair** and **CocoWalk** (see Shopping). Cafes line **Commodore Plaza** and the north end of **Main Highway**, while interesting boutiques are tucked into **Fuller Street**. The Grove, as it's popularly known, also hosts a celebrated Saturday farmers' market and street fairs throughout the year.

Key Biscayne

Key Biscayne (www.keybiscayne chamber.org) lies just 2mi south of downtown Miami but enjoys a much slower pace as well as a wealth of natural beauty. A haven for water sports and cyclists, this 7mi-long barrier island caught the public's attention when President Richard Nixon bought a vacation home here in the 1970s. The northern end is home to the **Miami Seaquarium★** (see Animal Parks), while the southern tip holds two popular beachfront parks, **Crandon Park** and **Bill Baggs Cape Florida State Park★** (see Beaches). Head west on the causeway toward Miami for spectacular **views★** of downtown.

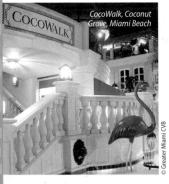

CocoWalk, Coconut Grove, Miami Beach

© Greater Miami CVB

You'll need at least a day to explore South Beach—a few hours to tour the Art Deco District, another few to browse in shops and galleries, and yet another few to linger in sidewalk cafes and people-watch. That's a bare minimum, of course—you'd have to spend far longer here to really soak up the scene. There are metered on-street parking spaces (*quarters only; 2hr limit strictly enforced*), but you'd be better off putting your car in a surface lot or garage and spending the day on foot. Stop by the **Miami Beach Visitors Center** (*1920 Meridian Ave.; daily 10am–4pm; 305-672-1270, ext 100 or 305-673-7400; www.miamibeachvisitorscenter.com*) to get information and advice; a moving **Holocaust Memorial** by artist Kenneth Treister stands across the street. Walking, bicycling, and self-guided audio tours of the Art Deco District are led by the **Miami Design Preservation League**, which also runs a terrific gift shop with all things Deco at its welcome center (*1001 Ocean Dr. at 10th St.; Mon–Sat 10am–4pm; 305-672-2014; www.mdpl.org*).

MIAMI BEACH★★★

One of the country's great tropical paradises, Miami Beach (pop. 87,933) is justifiably famed for its fabulous palm-studded shoreline, Art Deco architecture and colorful local residents. Built on dreams and speculation, this is an island in perpetual transition, where the atmosphere can shift from shabby to chic in a single block.

Today, Miami Beach and particularly its SoBe (South Beach) quarter are hotter than ever, with a sizzling nightlife and celebrity-studded cafes, clubs and beaches. A separate community from Miami, the City of Miami Beach occupies a narrow barrier island (7mi long and 1.5mi wide) 2.5mi off the mainland, along with 16 islets scattered in Biscayne Bay. The famous **South Beach** area (*below 23rd St.*) and the **Art Deco Historic District★★★** can be reached directly by the MacArthur Causeway.

While in town, be sure to check out **1111 Lincoln Road** (*1111lincolnroad.com*), a dazzling

Miami Beach

© Gino Santa Maria/Dreamstime.com

CITIES

new retail/residential space and parking garage, designed by Swiss architects Herzog & de Meuron. Save time to browse Miami Beach's two fine museums, the **Bass Museum of Art**★ and the **Wolfsonian–FIU**★★ (*see Museums for both*), the latter distinguished by the fanciful fountain in its lobby. Then relax on some of the best strips of sand in the state (*see Beaches*).

Art Deco Historic District★★★

This enclave of small-scale Art Deco hotels and apartment houses dating from the late 1920s to the early 1940s amounts to the largest concentration of architecture of its kind in the world. Some 36 hotels and 110 apartment buildings were constructed in the style in 1936 alone! The official district measures about one square mile and is roughly bounded by the Atlantic Ocean on the east, Lenox Avenue on the west, Sixth Street on the south and Dade Boulevard along the Collins Canal to the north. Celebrity-spotting is a prime pastime here in SoBe (local slang for South Beach), but the real stars are the buildings themselves.

Architectural Heritage

After several decades of decline, renewed interest in the Art Deco style was kindled by a retrospective of the International Exposition of Modern Decorative and Industrial Arts, held in Paris in 1925. A decade later, **Barbara Baer Capitman** and **Leonard Horowitz**, two local design professionals, formed the Miami Design Preservation League to identify significant architecture

in Miami Beach. The area's 1979 designation as a National Register Historic District was remarkable in that the roughly 800 Art Deco buildings included were only about 40 years old—not of an age typically considered historic. Many Art Deco buildings tend to have an angular look, with symmetrical, stepped-back facades and strong vertical banding and bas-relief decoration. (The ubiquitous pastel hues in Miami Beach are somewhat controversial, as the original buildings were white with trim painted in primary colors.) The later **Streamline Moderne** style featured aerodynamic imagery, horizontal racing stripes and wraparound corners, reflecting a fascination with speed and motion.

🏖 Ocean Drive★★

Both styles can be found all around the district but especially on Ocean Drive, the beating heart of the SoBe scene and home to many of its hottest dance clubs and bars. Here a pastel parade of Art Deco hotels, many with sidewalk cafes that are great for people watching, overlooks fabulous Ocean Beach. Note especially the **Tides** at no. 1220, the former **Leslie** hotel at no. 1244, and the **Cardozo** at no. 1250 (now owned by singer Gloria Estefan). The Streamline Moderne **Beach Patrol Station** at no. 1001 is home of the Miami Design Preservation League.

PALM BEACH★★★

A haven for the rich for more than a century, **Palm Beach** (pop. 10,468) occupies the northern part of a 16-mile-long barrier island and harbors one of the highest

The Other Palm Beach

Across the Intracoastal Waterway lies **West Palm Beach★** (pop. 89,905), whose lack of a true downtown hub was somewhat filled by CityPlace in 2000. The popular open-air mall, modeled on a European village, has 100 shops and restaurants (mostly chains) as well as a cineplex. A more compelling reason to visit West Palm is the fine **Norton Museum of Art★★** (*See Museums*).

concentrations of multimillion-dollar mansions in the world. Indeed, an air of exclusivity pervades just about everything about the place, from the gates and 20ft high hedges around many homes to the white-stucco banks that serve only "private" investors. Still, it's a fun day trip to shop and eat on or around Worth Avenue, spend some hours on the beach (yes, it's public!), see some art, and grab a drink at the world-famous **Breakers** resort—a luxurious old-school place to lay your head if you can afford it (*see Hotels*). You can get all the visitor information you need at: *www.palmbeachfl.com.*
When a Spanish schooner wrecked

off this coast in 1879, the area's few settlers happily inherited a windfall cargo of coconuts. They planted the spoils and met with surprising success: a flourishing grove of around 20,000 coconut palms that gave rise to the city's name. The lush, subtropical shoreline caught the eye of railroad and real estate tycoon **Henry M. Flagler** as he was scouting out a site for a new resort town in the late 19C. The Breakers and the **Flagler Museum★★** (*see Museums*), the latter housed in his former residence, are all that are left of his tenure here, but he would be pleased to know that Palm Beach remains a picture-perfect place of immaculately clean streets and opulent houses. For a look at some of the grandest ones, drive the stretch of **Ocean Boulevard** from Southern Boulevard to Barton Avenue, where it dead-ends. Continue one block west to **Bethesda-by-the-Sea★★** *(141 S. County Rd.)*, a Gothic Revival cast-stone Episcopal church (1927) whose tidy appearance is totally in keeping with the neighborhood.

BOCA RATON★

Situated halfway between Fort Lauderdale and West Palm Beach, sun-soaked Boca Raton (pop. 86,600) has catered to the well-heeled for more than 70 years. Drive down Aurelia, Azalea, Hibiscus or Oleander Street for a glimpse of one of Boca's oldest neighborhoods, **Old Floresta**. Designed by flamboyant architect and developer **Addison Mizner**, the pleasantly shady district still boasts 29 original houses with red barrel-tile roofs and light-colored

CityPlace, West Palm Beach

©Palm Beach County CVB

Gondola in the Venice of America, Fort Lauderdale

© 2009 Greater Fort Lauderdale CVB

stucco walls. Mizner's most opulent creation was the former Cloister Inn, a 100-room Mediterranean Revival hotel (1926) that now forms the east wing of the lavish **Boca Raton Resort and Club** (*see Hotels*). In addition to 2mi of white-sand public beach, the **Boca Raton Museum of Art★** (*see Museums*), adjacent Mizner Park, and the surrounding restaurants and shops are worth a visit.

FORT LAUDERDALE★

The largest city of sprawling Broward County, **Fort Lauderdale** (pop. 152,397) is known as the "Venice of America" for containing 300mi of natural and artificial waterways and 40,000-plus registered yachts. **Port Everglades** is the world's third-largest crusie port, with close to three million people departing annually for Caribbean ports of call. The city's transformation from agricultural village to major-league tourist destination was spurred by the arrival in 1896 of Henry Flagler's Florida East Coast Railway, which stopped here en route to Miami. Fort Lauderdale's lively downtown **Arts and Sciences District**—bounded by E. Broward

Boulevard on the north, the New River on the south, and S.E. Third and S.W. Seventh avenues on the east and west – encompasses the **Museum of Art★**, the **Museum of Discovery and Science★★** (*see Museums for both*) and the **Broward Center for the Performing Arts** (*see Performing Arts*). The latter sits at the western terminus of **Riverwalk**, a tree-lined bricked esplanade that stretches along the north and south banks of the New River. Just east of downtown, trendy **Las Olas Boulevard** boasts a wide variety of shops, galleries and outdoor cafes *(between S.E. 6th and 11th Aves.)*.

Fort Lauderdale Visitor Information

Visit the **Greater Fort Lauderdale Convention and Visitors Bureau** *(100 E. Broward Blvd., 800-22-SUNNY; www.sunny.org)* for bounteous travel information about the city and environs. This industrious group will mail you free literature, maps and guides upon request and has even launched a handy free iPhone app, iVisitLauderdale, packed with basic info as well as real-time weather, special events and deals.

MUSEUMS

Flagler Museum★★

*1 Whitehall Way, Palm Beach.
Open year-round Tue–Sat 10am–
5pm, Sun noon–5pm. Closed major
holidays. $18 includes docent-led
or audio tour. 561-655-2833.
www.flaglermuseum.us .*

Florida railroad magnate and
Standard Oil partner **Henry
Morrison Flagler** built this
imposing 55-room mansion
overlooking Lake Worth in 1901
as a wedding gift for his third
wife. Dubbed Whitehall, it has
been restored to its Flagler-era
appearance with many of the
original furnishings and gilded
age accoutrements like carved
precious wood, crystal chandeliers,
and museum-grade paintings.
Flagler's private railcar, an 1896
chapel, and Palm Beach's oldest
extant cottage decorate the lawn.

HistoryMiami★★

*101 W. Flagler St., Miami.
Open year-round Tues–Fri 10am–
5pm, Sat–Sun noon–5pm. Closed
major holidays. $8. 305-375-1492.
www.historymiami.org.*

The region's most important
historical museum interprets South
Florida history as a crossroads of
the Americas. Several distinct
collections—archaeological
finds from the area, Seminole
Indian artifacts, early to mid-20C
domestic objects, and works of
aviation history, maritime history
and folk art—drive home the
point, along with mixed-media
presentations.

Museum of Discovery and Science★★

*401 S.W. 2nd St., Fort Lauderdale,
one block south of Broward Blvd.
Open year-round Mon–Sat 10am–
5pm, Sun noon–6pm. $11 ($9/child
2-12 years); IMAX theater $9 ($7/
child); combo tickets available.
954-467-6637. www.mods.org.*

You don't have to be a kid to enjoy
this hands-on museum. The three-
story facility boasts more than 200
interactive exhibits, beginning
with the fantastic **gravity clock** in
the atrium. **Powerful You** lets you
test your brain function, strength,
and overall performance. **Florida
EcoScapes** dominates the first
floor with a colorful coral reef, an
underground cave, and a walk-in
beehive. Other highlights include
**Runways to Rockets: Our Place
in Aerospace**, where you can put
on wings and step into a giant
wind tunnel to see what it feels
like to fly.

The Miami International Art Fair

Founded in 2010, the annual MIA (*www.mia-artfair.com*) has established itself
as one of the hottest international art fairs around, with curators, artists and
dealers wheeling and dealing for four days in mid-January. Exhibitors set up in
the Miami Beach Convention Center, but there are related events at galleries
and museums all over town. Check website and local listings for details.

MUSEUMS

Norton Museum of Art,
West Palm Beach

©Palm Beach County CVB

Norton Museum of Art★★

1451 S. Olive Ave., West Palm Beach. Open year-round Tue–Sat 10am–5pm (Thu 9pm), Sun 11am–5pm. $12. 561-832-5196. www.norton.org.

Founded in 1941 by steel tycoon **Ralph H. Norton** (1875–1953), this stellar collection now consists of over 7,000 pieces. Special emphasis is placed on 19C–20C American and European works and Chinese art from 1700 BC to the early 1900s. Highlights include its **French Impressionist** and **post-Impressionist** paintings and 20C **American art**.

The Wolfsonian – FIU★★

1001 Washington Ave., Miami Beach. Open year-round Thu–Tue noon–6pm (Fri 9pm). $7 (free Fri 6–9pm). 305-531-1001. www.wolfsonian.org.

Florida International University oversees the Mitchell Wolfson Collection, which boasts more than 70,000 pieces of **American and European decorative arts and crafts** dating from 1885 to 1945, as well as rare books, graphics, propaganda art, architectural models, sculpture, glass, ceramics and furniture. About 300 works are displayed at any time.

Bass Museum of Art★

2121 Park Ave., Miami Beach. Open year-round Wed–Sun noon–5pm. $8. 305-673-7530. www.bassmuseum.org.

Housed in an Art Deco former library, this important regional museum mixes it up with an eclectic permanent collection including European painting and sculpture from the 15C to present; 7C to 20C textiles; modern art from the Americas and Caribbean; and items related to local design.

Boca Raton Museum of Art★

501 Plaza Real, Boca Raton. Open year-round Tue–Fri 10am–5pm (Wed 9pm), Sat & Sun noon–5pm. $8. 561-392-2500. www.bocamuseum.org.

Set in Mizner Park, this cheery pink museum presents four shows concurrently, some borrowed from other museums, others culled from its permanent collection of pre-Columbian and African art, late-19C and early-20C European art, and contemporary works.

Lowe Art Museum★

1301 Stanford Dr., on University of Miami campus. Open year-round Tue–Sat 10am–4pm, Sun noon–4pm. $10. 305-284-3535. www.lowemuseum.org.

The museum's wide-ranging collection includes objects from the pre-Columbian and Greco-Roman periods, Renaissance and Baroque paintings, 19C–20C American paintings, Native American textiles and jewelry, and African and Asian art. The **Palley Pavilion** holds a stunning glass collection with masterpieces by Dale Chihuly and others, as well as 3-D art.

Miami Art Museum★

101 W. Flagler St., Miami. Open year-round Tue–Fri 10am–5pm, weekends noon–5pm. $8, second Sat each month free. 305-375-3000. www.miamiart museum.org.

Dedicated to presenting international art of the post-World War II era, the museum stages several major shows a year. Fall 2013 is the target date for the move to exciting new digs designed by Herzog & de Meuron in Museum Park. The permanent collection includes works by Christo, Alexander Calder, Jasper Johns, Robert Rauschenberg, Marcel Duchamp and Rufino Tamayo.

Morikami Museum and Japanese Gardens★

4000 Morikami Park Rd., Boca Raton. 12mi northwest of Boca Raton in Delray Beach. Open year-round Tue–Sun 10am–5pm. $12. 561-495-0233. www.morikami.org.

Named after prosperous pineapple farmer George Sukeji Morikami, this 200-acre complex pays homage to Japanese culture. Changing exhibits showcase

artifacts ranging from vintage toys to lacquerware, woodblock prints and textiles. Traditional koi ponds, waterfalls and a **bonsai garden** dot the grounds, and once a month you can watch an authentic Japanese **tea ceremony** (*call or see website for schedule*). There's also a tasty pan-Asian cafe on-site.

Museum of Art, Fort Lauderdale★

1 E. Las Olas Blvd., Fort Lauderdale. Open year-round Tue–Sat 11am–5pm (Thu 8pm), Sun noon–5pm. $10. 954-525-5500. www.moafnsu.org.

The museum owns over 5,000 pieces ranging from impressionist works to pop art but is best known for its collection of **CoBrA art★★**—the largest assemblage in the US. Born in Paris in 1948, the CoBrA movement consisted of Expressionists from Copenhagen, Brussels and Amsterdam who drew their inspiration from folk art and children's drawings.

Museum of Contemporary Art★

770 N.E. 125th St., North Miami. Open year-round Tue & Thu–Sat 11am–5pm, Wed 1pm–9pm, Sun noon–5pm. Last Fri each month 7pm–10pm Jazz at MOCA. $5. 305-893-6211. www.mocanomi.org.

What's new in the art world? Come here to find out. This cutting-edge institution has about 700 works in its permanent collection and hosts traveling shows. Plans to expand architect Charles Gwathmey's simple but elegant building are in the works.

MUSEUMS

HISTORIC SITES

Vizcaya★★★

3251 S. Miami Ave., Miami. Open year-round Wed–Mon 9:30am–4:30pm. $15. 305-250-9133. www.vizcayamuseum.com.

Comprising an ornate Italian Renaissance-style villa and formal gardens, Vizcaya ("elevated place" in Basque) occupies 35 acres overlooking the calm blue waters of Biscayne Bay. American industrialist **James Deering** (1859–1925) employed 1,000 workers and spent $15 million over two years to complete this stunning homage to European design in 1916. The mansion has 70 rooms of which 34 are open to the public; 15C to 19C antiques and art abound. Step outside to wander more than 10 acres of formal **gardens**, punctuated with statuary, fountains, a pool, and a small "casino" (garden house).

East Loggia, Vizcaya

© Bill Sumner for Vizcaya Museum and Gardens

On your self-guided tour, be sure to visit the **chapel of St. Bernard de Clairvaux**. Above the altar, two circular stained-glass windows represent two of only three known **telescopic windows** in existence. In the middle of the complex stands a **prayer well** composed of elements of an AD 1C Roman temple.

Ancient Spanish Monastery★★

16711 W. Dixie Hwy, North Miami Beach. Open year-round Mon–Sat 10am–4pm, Sun 11am–4pm. $8. 305-945-1461. www.spanishmonastery.com.

Nestled on a woodsy site, the Cloisters of St. Bernard of Clairvaux, a superb example of early Gothic architecture, was completed in the Spanish province of Segovia in 1141. Nearly eight centuries later it was disassembled and moved to the US by newspaper magnate **William Randolph Hearst**. But it took more than 25 years and $1.5 million to open the reconstructed cloisters to the public (in 1954).

Barnacle State Historic Park★★

3485 Main Hwy., Miami. Park ($2) open year-round Wed–Mon dawn–dusk. House open year-round Fri–Mon 9am–5pm. Guided house tours (1hr) 10am, 11:30am, 1pm, 2:30pm. $3. 305-442-6866. www.floridastateparks.org/thebarnacle.

This five-acre bayfront site preserves one of the last patches of tropical hardwood hammock in Coconut Grove, along with the 1891 home of Ralph Middleton Munroe, an accomplished sailor and yacht designer. Nicknamed "The Barnacle," for its octagonal center that tapers to a small open-air vent, the five-room,

Castle of Mystery

28655 S. Dixie Hwy., 30mi south of Miami. Open year-round Sun–Thu 8am–6pm Fri–Sat 8am–8pm. $12. 305-248-6345. www.coralcastle.com. Speculation and mystery surround **Coral Castle★**, a mansion and sculpture garden, which was crafted of more than 1,100 tons of coral rock (oolitic limestone) between 1923 and 1951 by Latvian immigrant Edward Leedskalnin. Only 5ft tall and 110 pounds, Leedskalnin didn't use machinery and, when questioned, would only say that he knew "the secret of the pyramids." Scientists still debate his methods. Most remarkable are the movable **Nine-Ton Gate**; the **Polaris Telescope**, a 25ft-high, 30-ton rock telescope aimed at the North Star; the 20ft-long **Florida Table**, carved in the shape of the state and surrounded by 10,000-pound coral rock chairs; and the two-story tower where he lived and worked.

hip-roofed structure still contains the original furnishings. The 1926 boathouse, showcasing Munroe's shipbuilding tools, is also open to visitors.

Bonnet House Museum and Gardens★

900 N. Birch Rd., Fort Lauderdale. Open year-round, house by guided tour only, Tue–Sat 10am–4pm, Sun noon–4pm. $20; grounds only, $10. 954-563-5393. www.bonnethouse.org.

Thirty-five acres of woods surround this sprawling two-story mansion, which domestic diva Martha Stewart recently visited for design inspiration. Artist **Frederic Clay Bartlett** (1873–1953) was both its designer and owner, and he created the 30-room 1920 structure in the style of a Caribbean plantation with equal attention to outdoor and indoor living spaces.
Filled with family heirlooms, the manse is fronted by a lagoon rimmed with stately Royal palms and its namesake Bonnet lilies. Also on the grounds are Bartlett's **studio** and an **orchid house**.

Stranahan House★

335 S.E. 6th Ave., Fort Lauderdale. Open year-round daily, by guided tour (45–60min) only 1pm, 2pm, 3pm. $12. 954-524-4736. stranahanhouse.org.

Airy and elegant, the two-story frame house skirted by wide verandas is Broward County's oldest building, and its most popular historical site. It was built on the banks of the New River in 1901 by **Frank Stranahan**, the area's first permanent white settler, on the site of the trading post he set up to serve settlers and Seminoles. The interior boasts double-beaded wall paneling expertly crafted from Dade County pine.

Courtesy of Visit Florida

Stranahan House

HISTORIC SITES

BEACHES

South Florida is renowned for its white sand beaches. For more on Miami and Key Biscayne beaches, visit: *www.miamiandbeaches.com/visitors/beaches.asp.*

South Beach★★★

Stretching from 5th to 21st streets in Miami Beach is the most glamorous of all South Florida's beaches, with a skimpily clad clientele of young, rich, beautiful and trendy sun worshipers. Lummus Park, whose sands were shipped in from the Bahamas, is the heart of the SoBe scene. The rainbow flag at 12th Street marks an unofficial gay section.

South Beach

© Greater Miami CVB

South of South Beach are two popular family-oriented beaches, **South Pointe Park** and **First Street Beach**; **Central Beach**, just north of South Beach between 21st Street and 46th Street, is also great for families. Farther north, aptly named **North Beach**, from 46th Street to 78th Street, is community centered, with an old-fashioned bandshell, while upscale **Bal Harbour** beach offers a palm-shaded jogging path.

🏄 The Strip★

Fort Lauderdale's famed strip of beach, which unfurls for 2mi along Atlantic Boulevard *(on A1A, from Sunrise Blvd. to Bahia Mar Yacht Basin)*, became known in the 1950s not only for its beauty but as the prime destination for thousands of party-hardy college students during their annual Spring Break. After 30 years of this, city officials began actively—and successfully—discouraging the practice, so that in recent years the Strip has become a far quieter, more relaxing place year-round.

Key Biscayne

Just 2mi south of downtown Miami, the barrier island of Key Biscayne has a number of excellent beaches. Lovely **Bill Baggs Cape Florida State Park★** *(1200 S. Crandon Blvd.; $8 per vehicle; 305-361-5811; www.floridastateparks. org/capeflorida)* offers a mile of Biscayne Bay beachfront, a 74-acre wetlands area, a bicycle trail, and tours *(Thu–Mon 10am & 1pm)* of the still operational 1825 **Cape Florida Lighthouse**. Three-mile-long **Crandon Park** beach *(4000 Crandon Blvd.; 305-361-5421)* caters to families with a carousel and playgrounds. **Hobie Beach/ Windsurfer Beach** *(south end)* is a long, palm-lined beach with views of the Miami skyline as well as rentals of kayaks, pedal boats, and windsurfing equipment. Long-shuttered **Virginia Key Beach Park** *(www.virginiakey beachpark.net)* reopened in 2008 to great fanfare, appealing to kids with a mini train ride and a vintage carousel, as well as a long stretch of white sand.

ANIMAL PARKS

Lion Country Safari★★

16mi west of I-95 on Southern Blvd., West Palm Beach. Open year-round daily 9:30am–5:30pm (ticket booths close at 4:30pm). $26.50 ($19.50/child 3-9). 561-793-1084. www.lioncountrysafari.com.

Watch more than 1,300 animals of 131 different species roam in this 500-acre, drive-through game preserve, home to such exotics as lowland tapirs, llamas and Aldabra tortoises from South America; lions, antelope, wildebeest, elephants, ostriches from Africa; and water buffalo native to India. There are seven habitats in all. Also onsite: boat and carousel rides, a water park and a petting zoo.

Zoo Miami★★

12400 S.W. 152nd St., 18mi from downtown Miami. Open year-round daily 9:30am–5:30pm (gates close at 4pm). $15.95, ($11.95/child 3-12 years). 305-251-0400. www.miamimetrozoo.com.

One of the finest zoos in the US, 290-acre Zoo Miami specializes in tropical species adaptable to South Florida's hot climate. Some 900 reptiles, birds and mammals, primarily from Asia, Africa and Australia live here. Camouflaged moats and other inconspicuous barriers separate visitors from the animals, which appear to roam free in natural habitats. Highlights include an affectionate band of **lowland gorillas** and a group of stunning **Bengal tigers**. The zoo also has a children's playground, a tropical free-flight aviary, and a giraffe feeding station.

Butterfly World, Coconut Creek

© Richard Nowitz/Apa Publications

Butterfly World★

Tradewinds Park, 3600 W. Sample Rd., Coconut Creek (10mi north of Fort Lauderdale). Open year-round Mon–Sat 9am–5pm, Sun 11am–5pm. $24.95 ($19.95/child 3-11). 954-977-4400. www.butterflyworld.com.

Take a lovely walk through a screened-in aviary, landscaped with waterfalls and bright blooms to resemble a tropical rainforest. Inside, some 10,000 butterflies and hundreds of birds flit around. Outside, a rose garden and vine-covered arbor surround a small pond, attracting local species of the order Lepidoptera.

Jungle Island★

1111 Parrot Jungle Trail, Miami. Open year-round daily 10am–5pm. $32.95 ($24.95/child 3-10). 305-400-7275. www.jungleisland.com.

More than 1,100 exotic birds, including some 80 pink flamingos, dwell at this popular spot on Biscayne Bay, where paths wind past a serpentarium, crocodile pond, aviary and penguinarium. Don't miss a show: **Winged Wonders** or **Tale of the Tiger**.

THE GREAT OUTDOORS

Fairchild Tropical Garden★★

10901 Old Cutler Rd., 10mi south of downtown Miami. Open year-round daily 9:30am–4:30pm. Narrated tram tours Mon–Fri 10am–3pm, weekends 10am–4pm. $25. 305-667-1651. www.fairchildgarden.org.

Set on 83 well-tended acres studded with 12 man-made lakes, the largest botanical garden in the continental US boasts more than 2,500 species of plants and trees from around the world.
The gardens, named for plant explorer David Fairchild, opened in 1938. Plants here are grouped by families and arranged in spaces that vary from narrow allées to open beds. A tram tour (*45min*) takes visitors past a sampling of the garden's flora, including 500 species of **palms** and a group of rare **cycads**, a species that dates from the Cretaceous period.

⚘ Venetian Pool★★

2701 DeSoto Blvd., Miami. Hours vary. $11. 305-460-5306. www.coralgablesvenetianpool.com.

A limestone quarry that supplied building materials for the area's early homes formed the base of this whimsical municipal pool. Working in tandem in 1922, artist Denman Fink and architect Phineas Paist concocted a fanciful design incorporating a casino, towers, striped light poles (like those lining Venice's Grand Canal) and footbridges that cross the free-form swimming area.

Arthur R . Marshall Loxahatchee National Wildlife Refuge★

8mi west of Boca Raton, on US-441. Open year-round daily sunrise–sunset. $5 per vehicle. 561-734-8303. www.fws.gov/loxahatchee.

Hike, camp, and canoe at this 221sq mi refuge at the northernmost tip of the Everglades, home to more than 18,000 alligators and numerous species of birds, including the endangered snail kite and wood stork. The visitor center (*daily 9am–4pm*) contains dioramas and exhibits on local ecology.

Biscayne National Park★

East end of N. Canal Dr. (S.W. 328th St.), Homestead; 38mi south of Miami. Open year-round daily 7am–5:30pm. 305-230-7275. www.nps.gov/bisc.

This is the largest marine park in the US, protecting a 275sq mi area of coastal wetlands, mangrove shorelines, coral reefs and 32 small barrier islands.
The **visitor center** has a number of fascinating exhibits, but the **reef★★★**, 10mi offshore, is the main attraction.
Here warm Gulf Stream currents nurture some 50 species of living coral that create a hospitable environment for loggerhead turtles, spiny lobsters, sponges and flamboyant tropical fish.
The park's concessionaire offers cruises and snorkeling and scuba excursions around Biscayne Bay (*www.BiscayneUnderwater.com*).

PERFORMING ARTS

Though hardly a hotbed for live performance, Miami and, to a lesser extent, other South Florida cities put on their share of concerts and theater. But cutting-edge music in architecturally distinct spaces is on the rise with the debut of the Arsht and the New World centers. To purchase tickets, contact the box office or **Ticketmaster** *(305-533-1361; www.ticketmaster.com).*

Adrienne Arsht Center for the Performing Arts
1300 Biscayne Blvd. 786-468-2000; box office: 305-949-6722. www.arshtcenter.org.
Designed by Cesar Pelli, the largest (570,000sq ft) and most vital performing arts venue in the state debuted in 2006. Companies in residence include the New World Symphony, the Miami City Ballet, and the Florida Grand Opera. The Arsht Center also sponsors many Latin performers as well as the Florida Grand Opera, the Miami City Ballet, and more in a truly fabulous space.

American Airlines Arena
601 Biscayne Blvd, Miami. 786-777-1000. www.aaarena.com.
Home of Miami Heat NBA basketball, the Arena also hosts concerts (Taylor Swift, Sade/John

American Airlines Arena

© Felix Miziozinikov/Dreamstime.com

Legend) and other large-venue events (Cirque de Soleil, Disney on Ice) as well as more intimate performances in the Waterfront Theater.

Broward Center for the Performing Arts
201 SW Fifth Ave, Ft Lauderdale. 954-462-0222 or 877-311-7469. www.browardcenter.org.
Home to four theaters of varying

Spectator Sports

South Floridians are proud of their sports teams, and for good reason. The aptly named **Miami Heat** pro basketball team has been on fire since snagging forward LeBron James from the Cleveland Cavaliers in 2010 *(786-777 -HOOP; www.nba.com/heat)*. In Major League Baseball, the **Florida Marlins** have won the World Series twice, in 1997 and 2003—the only two times they made it to the postseason—despite only becoming a team in 1993. In 2012 they'll be known as the Miami Marlins when they move into their new $515-million ballpark on the site of the former Orange Bowl *(877-MARLINS; florida.marlins.mlb.com)*. The National Football League's **Miami Dolphins**, a formidable team in the 1970s to 1990s, have been lackluster for the past decade *(888-FINS-TIX; www.miamidolphins.com)*.

sizes, the complex anchors the west end of Fort Lauderdale's Riverwalk Arts & Entertainment District and stages a mix of theater, music, dance and family entertainment.

Byron Carlyle Theater
500 71st St., Miami Beach. 305-674-1040. www.colonyand byrontheaters.com.
This intimate 304-seat theater now serves as the premier performing-arts venue in North Miami Beach, hosting a wide variety of music, dance, theater, comedy and film.

Colony Theater
1040 Lincoln Rd, Miami Beach. 305-674-1040. www.colonyand byrontheaters.com.
This Art Deco landmark opened in 1935 as a Paramount Pictures movie palace. Now restored to its former glory – the Colony celebrated its 75th anniversary in 2010 – the theater plays host to all manner of eclectic live performances from music to comedy to film.

Fillmore Miami Beach at Jackie Gleason Theater
1700 Washington Ave, Miami Beach. 305-673-7300; www.gleasontheater.com.
Known for hosting Gleason, Jack Benny and Bob Hope, this venerable theater today hosts rock concerts along with the Miami City Ballet and the Miami Beach Broadway Series. Look for the handprints and signatures of celebrities such as Chita Rivera, Julie Andrews and *Miami Vice* star Don Johnson in the **Walk of Stars** outside the box office entrance.

New World Center
500 17th St., Miami Beach. 305-673-3331. www.nws.edu.
Frank Gehry designed the boxy new digs for the New World Symphony, founded by conductor Michael Tilson Thomas. Covered with white stuccoed concrete, the structure hosted its inaugural concert in January 2011 in its acoustically marvelous 756-seat performance hall. A 7000sq ft outdoor projection screen and a garden wired for first-rate sound set the scene for memorable alfresco concerts.

Olympia Theater at the Gusman Center for the Performing Arts
174 E Flagler Street, Miami. 305-374-2444. www.gusmancenter.org.
This magnificently restored theater, which opened in 1926 as a silent-movie palace, earned oohs and aahs with its striking Moorish architecture and simulated night sky inside. Still boasting perfect acoustics, the venue is now home to live performances, film screenings and community events. Some of the glitterati who have played the Gusman over the years include Elvis Presley, B.B. King and Luciano Pavarotti.

Olympia Theater at the Gusman Center for the Performing Arts

Olympia Theater at Gusman Center for the

SHOPPING

Worth Avenue ★★
Between Ocean Blvd. and Cocoanut Row, Palm Beach. Check online for hours: www.worth-avenue.com.

The East Coast's answer to Rodeo Drive in Beverly Hills, California, this upscale street draws well-heeled shoppers, who come to eat and browse at such fashion pacesetters as Cartier, Louis Vuitton, Chanel and Loro Piana. In 1924, developer Addison Mizner designed the delightful alleyways, such as **Via Mizner★**, which thread off the main road into charming courtyards of tile-work fountains and hanging flower baskets.

Bayside Marketplace★
401 Biscayne Blvd., R106, Miami. Mon–Thu 10am–10pm, Fri & Sat 10am–11pm, Sun 11am–9pm. 305-577-3344. www.bayside marketplace.com.

Linked to the north side of Bayfront Park via sidewalk, this popular complex comprises several buildings connected by plazas and open-air walkways overlooking the turquoise waters of Biscayne Bay. Its profusion of boutiques, retail outlets, eateries and entertainment sprawls over 235,000sq ft and lures visitors with its bequiling ambience and vibrant nightlife.

Bal Harbour Shops
9700 Collins Ave., Bal Harbour. Mon–Sat 10am–9pm, Sun noon–6pm. 305-866-0311. www.bal harbourshops.com.

Upscale alfresco shopping is found in what was Miami's first luxury shopping mall beyond the city. It's now a mecca of high-fashion stores and boutiques such as Neiman Marcus, Saks Fifth Avenue, Louis Vuitton, Prada and Bulgari.

Cocowalk
3015 Grand Ave., Coconut Grove. Sun–Thu 10am–10pm, Fri & Sat 10am–11pm. 305-444-0777. www.cocowalk.net.

Leave it to Coconut Grove, South Florida's center of eclectic eccentricity, to create a fantasy of bars, theaters and specialty retailers that stand out for their variety and style. Pink stucco and three levels of loggias and balconies give the mall a cheerful tropical air.

Galleria Mall
2414 E. Sunrise Blvd., Ft Lauderdale. Mon–Sat 10am–9pm, Sun noon–6pm. 954-564-1015. www.galleriamall-fl.com.

Originally known as the Sunrise Shopping Center until its 1980 redevelopment, The Galleria is now the largest upscale regional shopping center in Broward County. High-end anchor Neiman Marcus is joined by the likes of Apple, Coach, Williams-Sonoma, J.Crew and Pottery Barn

Lincoln Road Mall
1610 Lenox Ave., Miami Beach. Mon–Sat 10am–9pm, Sun noon–6pm. 305-534-9857. lincolnroadmall.com.

Chock-a-block with trendy retailers, art galleries, coffee shops and restaurants, this beautifully landscaped pedestrian mall is one of the best spots to shop and dine in sexy South Beach.

NIGHTLIFE

With more than 100 clubs to choose from, South Beach is unquestionably the center of Miami's "American Riviera" café society. For the non-celebrities among us, access to the club of your dreams can be a challenge. Some hotels offer services to help you bypass the velvet ropes; check with the concierge for VIP passes or other tips.

Liv

Fonteainbleau Miami Beach, 4441 Collins Ave., Miami Beach. 305-674 -4680. www.livnightclub.com.
Creating a distinctly 21st-century vibe in one of Miami Beach's most historic entertainment sites, the famed Fonteainbleau, this bold venue features more than 18,000sq ft of excitement. With a design that offers tantalizing glimpses of VIPs and celebrities, this is the place to see and be seen.

Mansion

1235 Washington Ave., Miami Beach. 305-695-8411. www.mansionmiami.com.
Currently holding Miami's "hottest club" status with A-list celebrities in abundance, Mansion is both sleek and opulent. Its dance floor, top-of-the-line powerhouse sound system, plexiglass video screens and dramatic lighting enhanced by sumptuous suede and leather furnishings create an unforgettable experience.

Art Walks

Not into the club scene? For the culturally inclined, Miami's arts community offers a vibrant calendar of Art Walks in communities throughout the city, including brad/FAD (the Bird Road Art District/Fashion Art District), Brickell Avenue, Coconut Grove, Coral Gables, Little Havana, the Design District and Wynwood. Get the lowdown at *artcircuits.com*.

Mynt Lounge

1921 Collins Ave., Miami Beach. 305-532-0727. www.mynt lounge.com.
Exclusive Mynt Lounge claims the "tightest door policy in town," so be prepared to compete for entry here. It's not the newest club, but there's something about the place that keeps 'em coming back; so put on a high-wattage smile and go for it!

Nikki Beach

One Ocean Dr., Miami Beach. 305-538-1111. www.nikkibeach miami.com.
The Miami version of this international brand offers palm trees and ocean breezes, creating a setting that is both casual and exclusive. The hot NB club scene is balanced with plenty of places to retreat for more intimate conversation.

Nighttime on Ocean Drive, Miami Beach

© Fotografie K.J. Schraa/ iStockphoto.com

MUST DO

SPAS

The resort atmosphere and the emphasis on youth, fitness and style that characterize the Miami and South Florida make it a natural fit for the spa culture. An annual Spa Month (www.miamispamonth.com) is actually a two-month period, July 1 to August 31, when local spas promote their services through special offers.

Canyon Ranch
6801 Collins Avenue, Miami Beach. 305-514-7000 or 800-742-9000. www.canyonranch.com/ miamibeach.
For years the name Canyon Ranch has represented the epitome of fitness, nutrition and glowing health. This spa in the elegantly restored Carillon Hotel, an icon of 1950s Miami Modern architecture, offers a sumptuous array of massage therapies, body treatments, and facials as well as the signature Aquavana thermal program.

Exhale
EPIC Residences + Hotel, 270 Biscayne Blvd. Way, Miami. 305 423 3900. www.exhalespa.com.
Fusion massage, a four-hand massage, and a "glow" treatment featuring dry-brush, citrus-sugar scrub and moisturizing lotion are among the soothing services offered at Exhale's two locations (the other at Omphoy Ocean Resort in Palm Beach.

Mandarin Oriental Spa
500 Brickell Key Dr., Miami, 305-913-8288. www.mandarin oriental.com/Miami.
From a full menu of spa services, choose such luxuries as the Oriental Essence massage, targeting neck and shoulder tension, or the Sun Ritual body wrap to relieve the drying effects of the South Florida sun.

The Ritz-Carlton Key Biscayne Spa
415 Grand Bay Dr, Key Biscayne. 305-648-5900. www.ritz carlton.com.
This 20,000-square-foot West Indies colonial-style setting rolls out more than 60 treatments, including the Key Lime Coconut Body Scrub and the Everglades Grass Body Wrap. The Fountain of Youth treatment is a six-hour indulgence.

The Spa at Conrad Miami
1395 Brickell Ave., Miami. 305-503-6500. www.conrad hotels1.hilton.com.
The Conrad's spa customizes massage and skin treatments (such as a collagen-infused mask) to soothe your senses, whether it's only for an hour, a full day, or a relaxing getaway weekend.

The Spa at PGA National Resort
450 Ave. of the Champions, Palm Beach Gardens. 800-843-7725. www.thespaatpga national.com.
Plunge yourself into a heated mineral pool, relax with a seaweed facial mask or pamper yourself with a reflexology pedicure at this lavish resort. You can even schedule cosmetic procedures here, performed by a board-certified plastic surgeon.

NORTHEAST COAST

Motorists once raced through this corner of the state on their way south, but more and more travelers are discovering the myriad charms of the 125-mile strand from Fernandina Beach to Daytona Beach. Long heralded for historic St. Augustine and boisterous Daytona Beach, northeast Florida also claims its own sea islands (the southern part of Georgia's famous barrier-island chain).

The First Coast

Spanish explorer Ponce de León claimed northeast Florida for Spain in 1513. A permanent settlement was founded, at **St. Augustine★★★**, in 1565. Except for a brief British occupation, St. Augustine remained Spanish for the next 256 years, until Spain handed Florida over to the US in 1821. Soon afterward, 30mi north on the banks of the St. Johns River, **Jacksonville★** was established, rising to prominence as a port and tourist town.

By the end of the 19C, Jacksonville's days as Florida's premier visitor destination were over, thanks largely to **Henry Flagler's** Florida East Coast Railway, which opened up St. Augustine and other sunny spots farther south. In recent times, Jacksonville has reinvigorated its tourist offerings with art museums, a landscaped riverwalk and fine beaches. St. Augustine remains a bastion of history with its red-tile roofs, quaint courtyards, 17C coquina (shell stone) buildings, and charming B&Bs.

Another magnet for tourists in this region, particularly during Spring Break, is **Daytona Beach**, famous for its long sandy strip and fast cars. Less well known is picturesque **Amelia Island★★**, an ideal place for just kicking back.

Practical Information

When to Go

Unlike South Florida, Northeast Florida enjoys the four seasons, so plan your beach time accordingly. Jacksonville's average daytime temperatures are as follows: January, 53F/12C; April, 69F/21C; July, 82F/28C; October 70F/21C.

Getting There and Around

◆ **Jacksonville International Airport (JAX)**, 15mi north of city, is the main airport in the region (*904-741-4902; www.jia.aero*). **Public transport, taxis**, and **rental-car** agencies are onsite.

◆ Jacksonville's **Amtrak** station is at *3570 Clifford Lane;* St. Augustine's is 45min away in Palatka (*800-USA-RAIL; www.amtrak.com*). To get around and between cities, a car is recommended.

Visitor Information

Visit *www.floridashistoriccoast.com* for details on St. Augustine and area beaches.

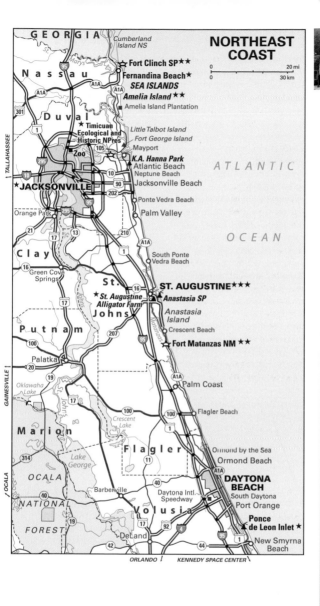

GEORGIA

Cumberland Island NS

N a s s a u

☆ Fort Clinch SP★★
Fernandina Beach★
SEA ISLANDS
Amelia Island ★★
■ Amelia Island Plantation

D u v a l

★ Timucuan
Ecological and
Historic NPres
Little Talbot Island
Fort George Island
Mayport
K.A. Hanna Park ●
Atlantic Beach
Neptune Beach
Jacksonville Beach

Zoo

★**JACKSONVILLE**

A T L A N T I C

○ Ponte Vedra Beach

Orange Park

○ Palm Valley

C l a y

Green Cove
Springs

O C E A N

○ South Ponte
Vedra Beach

S t .

ST. AUGUSTINE★★★
★ St. Augustine
Alligator Farm
Anastasia SP

J o h n s

*Anastasia
Island*
○ Crescent Beach

P u t n a m

★ Fort Matanzas NM ★★

Palatka

*Oklawaha
Lake*

◐ Palm Coast

● Flagler Beach

M a r i o n

*Crescent
Lake*

*Lake
George*

F l a g l e r

Ormond by the Sea
Ormond Beach

OCALA

Barberville

Daytona Intl.
Speedway
**DAYTONA
BEACH**
South Daytona
Port Orange

NATIONAL

V o l u s i a

**Ponce
de Leon Inlet ★**

FOREST

DeLand

New Smyrna
Beach

ORLANDO /   *KENNEDY SPACE CENTER *

**NORTHEAST
COAST**

| 0 | | 20 mi |
| 0 | | 30 km |

| TALLAHASSEE
| GAINESVILLE
/ OCALA

NORTHEAST COAST

75

CITIES

St. Augustine★★★

The oldest continuously occupied European settlement in the US, **St. Augustine** (pop. 12,263) is sure to charm you with its narrow, cobbled lanes, fascinating history museums and Gilded Age resort hotels. The small city lies on Florida's east coast, 33mi south of Jacksonville, on a finger of land extending south from the mainland between the Matanzas and San Sebastián rivers. Spanish commander **Pedro Menéndez de Avilés** first dropped anchor here in 1565 on a mission to rout nearby French Huguenots. The town flipped back and forth between Spanish and British hands before finally becoming part of the US in 1821. While stories proclaiming this spot as the landing site of Ponce de León in his search for the mythical Fountain of Youth are apocryphal, the city's archaeological importance is unquestioned. In recent decades, researchers have uncovered artifacts and building foundations at the **Fountain of Youth Archaeological Park** *(155 Magnolia Ave.; 904-829-3168 or 800-356-8222; www.fountainof youthflorida.com)* that indicate the Menendez's presence, as well as the probable location of the Timucuan village of Seloy, home to the Indians who welcomed him.

Historic District

After checking out the **Castillo de San Marcos★★★**, stop in at the visitor center *(10 W. Castillo Dr.; 904-825-1000; www.staugustine government.com)* to get the scoop on tours, special events, and the like. (The center's huge lot is a good place to park.) From there, it's only a few steps to the **Old City Gate**, two 1808 coquina (shell stone) pillars that mark the entrance to **St. George Street**, the backbone of the old city. Historic houses and museums abound throughout the quarter *(see Museums and Historic Sites for the best ones)*.

Henry Morrison Flagler

Tourists started coming en masse to St. Augustine shortly after Henry Flagler did. The son of a Presbyterian minister, Flagler (1830-1913) was born in Hopewell, New York, left school at 14, and developed a knack for salesmanship in Ohio that led him to a partnership with the wealthy industrialist John D. Rockefeller. Their oil refinery incorporated in 1870 as Standard Oil.

Flagler spent his second honeymoon in St. Augustine in 1883, observing that while its warm climate drew wealthy winter visitors, the city offered few amenities. Five years later he opened his luxurious **Ponce de Leon Hotel** (now **Flagler College★★**) and the **Hotel Alcazar** (now the **Lightner Museum★★**). Even more shrewdly, he improved the railroad linking St. Augustine with the rest of the Eastern Seaboard, so that wealthy urbanites could get here with ease. Gradually he extended his Florida East Coast Railway all the way to the Keys. Development along the line exploded, as did Flagler's wealth. Upon his death, his remains were interred at St. Augustine's Memorial Presbyterian Church, which he had commissioned in 1889.

Jacksonville★

Anchored by the north-flowing St. Johns River, Jacksonville (pop. 790,689) is the largest city in the US—in terms of area, at least—extending over 840 square miles of Florida's northeastern corner. For visitors, though, the downtown area and beaches area are the places to be, so the city never really feels that big. Jacksonville is also a popular jumping-off point for the **Sea Islands**, which aside from the requisite abundance of sand and sea (*See Beaches*) sport several historic areas, including the **Centre Street Historic District★** in the town of **Fernandina Beach★** on the north end of Amelia Island.

Downtown – North

Most of Jacksonville's attractions are crowded along the north side of the St. Johns River. Start at the **visitor center** *(904-791-4305; www.visitjacksonville.com)* on the lower level of **Jacksonville Landing★**, a shopping and entertainment complex (*see Shopping*).

Just a few blocks north stands the **Museum of Contemporary Art** *(333 N. Laura St., 904-366-6911; www.mocajacksonville.org)*, housed on five floors of a former Western Union building (1931).

Cummer Museum of Art and Gardens

Photo Courtesy of Visit Florida

Then head over to the **Riverside/Avondale Historic District★**, where you'll find a plethora of residential architectural styles, a park designed by Frederick Law Olmsted, and the remarkable **Cummer Museum of Art and Gardens★★** (*See Museums*).

Downtown – South

The mile-long **Riverwalk** on the south side of the river offers some of the best views of the river and the north bank. And in Friendship Park just west of the Main Street Bridge stands the **Museum of Science and History★** (*see Museums*).

Daytona Beach

Gateway to a 26-mile stretch of hard-packed sandy **beach★★**, this sun-splashed resort town (pop. 66,465) has long been known for college kids on Spring Break and stock-car races. But more recently, Daytona Beach has begun to court vacationing families with new attractions and upscale hotels. Roughly 11mi south of downtown, the **Ponce de Leon Inlet Lighthouse★** *(386-761-1821; www.ponceinlet.org)*, an 1887 beacon that is one of the most complete light stations in Florida, makes for a fun side trip. Climb the 203 steps for breathtaking **views★★**.

CITIES

77

The Daytona 500

NASCAR's biggest and most prestigious race, the Daytona 500, got its start here on February 22, 1959, with a field of 59 cars vying for $67,760 in prize money. Some 41,000 fans turned out to watch **Lee Petty** in the 200-lap contest that ended in a photo finish. Today, the crowd at the annual event tops 161,000 and the prize money is around $18 million. Cars travel at speeds of up to 190mph, taking curves banked at 31 degrees.

Lee's son **Richard Petty** dominates the record books here, with the most victories as well as the most miles driven at Daytona. Another racing legend, **Dale Earnhart**, started the race 20 times before finally hoisting the victory trophy in 1998. If you're not lucky enough to be here for a race (and there are many others aside from the Daytona 500), you can drop by the speedway for a track tour ranging from 30 minutes (Speedway) to 3 hours (VIP). Tours are held daily on a first-come, first-served basis except during events (*877-306-RACE; www.daytonainternationalspeedway.com*).

Main Street Pier

A 20ft-wide concrete walkway with benches and telescopes, Boardwalk extends three blocks north from Main Street to Ora Street along Daytona's beach. The 1,000ft-long pier dates from 1925. Tourists young and old gravitate to this area, encountering a seaside bazaar of video arcades and fishing rentals, as well as the heart-stopping **Sling-Shot**, which launches you 300ft into the air at 100mph.

For the best view of the beach, ascend to the top of the 180ft **Space Needle** at the end of the pier.

MUSEUMS

Cummer Museum of Art and Gardens★★

829 Riverside Ave., Jacksonville. Open year-round Tue–Fri 10am–4pm (Tue 9pm), Sat 10am–5pm, Sun noon–5pm. Closed major holidays. $10 (free Tue 4pm–9pm). 904-356-6857. www.cummer.org.

With its remarkable riverfront setting, the Cummer boasts a reputation as one of Florida's best small art museums. Opened in 1961, the museum stands on the site of the former home of Jacksonville residents Arthur and Ninah Cummer, incorporating the original Italian and English formal gardens, as well as the mahogany-paneled **Tudor Room**. Through acquisitions and gifts, the collection has expanded to more than 6,000 works of American and European art encompassing 8,000 years of history.

Lightner Museum★★

75 King St., St. Augustine. Open year-round daily 9am–5pm. $10. 904-824-2874. www.lightner museum.org.

Housed in Henry Flagler's massive former Hotel Alcazar is a diverse assortment of decorative arts and collectibles, including art glass that belonged to the museum's namesake, **Otto C. Lightner**, a Chicago publisher who purchased the hotel building in 1946.

Museum of Arts and Sciences★

1040 Museum Blvd., Daytona Beach. Open Tue–Sat & holidays Mon 9am–5pm, Sun 11am–5pm. $12.95; children 6-17 $6.95. 386-255-0285. www.moas.org.

An affiliate of the Smithsonian Institution, this museum is located on the Tuscawilla Preserve, where a raised boardwalk offers hiking trails. American popular culture stars in the **Root Family Museum**; a pre-history wing showcases a 130,000- year-old giant ground sloth **skeleton**; the **Cuban art** collection chronicles life in Cuba from 1759-1959; while the **African art** gallery presents objects from 30 different cultures.

Also onsite is a hands-on **children's museum** and free **planetarium shows**.

Museum of Science and History and Planetarium★

1025 Museum Circle, Jacksonville. Open year-round Mon–Thu, 10am–5pm, Fri 10am–8pm, Sat 10am–6pm, Sun 1pm–6pm. Closed major holidays. $10 (children 3-12). $8. 904-396-6674. www.themosh.org.

History is adventure and science is fun at this hands-on museum near the foot of Main Street Bridge. Exhibits explore natural and physical sciences, regional natural history and north Florida's past. The **Alexander Brest Planetarium** boasts a state-of-the-art sound system staging multimedia shows daily. Shows are free with admission.

HISTORIC SITES

⚜ Castillo de San Marcos National Monument★★★

1 S. Castillo Dr., St. Augustine. Open year-round daily 8:45am–5:15pm (6:15pm in summer). $6. 904-829-6506. www.nps.gov/casa.

Defender of St. Augustine since the beginning of the 18C, the oldest masonry fort in the US overlooks Matanzas Bay at the northern boundary of the old city. The Castillo withstood every enemy attack that beset it and today ranks among the best-preserved examples of Spanish Colonial fortifications in the

New World. Rooms around the interior courtyard contain displays describing the fort's history. Stoop to enter a low passageway to the powder magazine, then continue up the stairs to the **gundeck**,

Photo Courtesy of Visit Florida

Cannon, Castillo de San Marcos

where the original cannons are fired throughout the day. The **view** from here demonstrates the ease with which sentries could monitor an intruder's approach.

Cathedral-Basilica of St. Augustine★★

North side of Plaza de la Constitución, St. Augustine. Open daily 9am–4:30pm. 904-824-2806. www.thefirstparish.org.

The parish of St. Augustine, founded c.1565, ranks as the oldest Catholic parish in the US. Not until 1793 did diocesan authorities commission a permanent coquina structure north of the plaza. An 1887 fire destroyed all but the walls and facade. Massive decorated timbers support the ceiling above floors of Cuban tile. A large, ornamental reredos of gold and white wood, incorporating the marble altar from the original church, highlights the sanctuary.

Fort Clinch State Park★★

2601 Atlantic Ave., Fernandina Beach (on the north end of Amelia Island). Open daily 9am–5pm; $6/vehicle. 904-277-7274. www.florida stateparks.org/fortclinch.

This splendid expanse offers access to a wide beach, a fishing pier and nature trails; its centerpiece is a brick fort dating from the 1840s. Displays in the visitor center outline US defense systems prior to 1840 and detail the construction of the fort. From the center, a short path leads to the fort, its massive pentagonal walls interrupted only by a wooden drawbridge. Visitors are free to roam the four-acre

interior or to climb the ramparts for a **view** of Cumberland Island.

Fort Matanzas National Monument★★

15mi south via A1A, on Matanzas River south of Crescent Beach, St. Augustine. Open year-round daily 9am–5:30pm. 904-471-0116. www.nps.gov/foma.

The 300-acre park preserves a coquina tower erected in 1742 to defend Matanzas Inlet. Matanza means slaughter in Spanish, recalling how, in 1565, some 300 French Huguenot soldiers and settlers were massacred here by the forces of Pedro Menéndez de Avilés. Watch a short film about the fort's history in the visitor center, then board a ferry to see fort itself. Back on the mainland, a trail leads to the site of the massacre.

Gonzalez-Alvarez House (The Oldest House)★★

14 St. Francis St., St. Augustine. Open year-round daily 9am–5pm. $8. 904-824-2872. www.staugustine historicalsociety.org.

This museum complex includes Florida's oldest house, two museums, an exhibition gallery, a garden and a store. The handsome Gonzalez-Alvarez dwelling is thought to be St. Augustine's oldest extant residential structure. Tour guides explain the history of the house, vividly evoking life in colonial Florida. Take a walk in the ornamental **garden** where you can see plants grown by colonists. The **Manucy Museum**, in the 1924 Webb Building, presents over 400 years of Florida's history, while the **Page L. Edwards Gallery** mounts changing historical exhibitions.

Ximenez-Fatio House★★

20 Aviles St., St. Augustine. Visit by guided tour only, year-round Mon–Sat 11am–4pm. $7. 904-829-3575. www.ximenezfatiohouse.org.

This two-story coquina residence offers a look at the way early St. Augustine buildings were adapted for various uses. It was built in 1798 by Spanish merchant Andrés Ximenez as his residence and general store. Under a later owner, the establishment thrived as the city's most popular inn from the mid- to late 19C. Today the house reflects the period 1830–1850.

Colonial Spanish Quarter★

33 St. George St., St. Augustine. Open year-round daily 9am–4:45pm (last admission). $7. www.staugustinegovernment.com.

This living-history museum re-creates the latter years of the city's first Spanish period. After entering through Florencia House, visitors may walk the grassy "streets" of St. Augustine c.1740. The dwellings of a foot soldier, an artillery sergeant and a cavalryman emphasize variations in wealth and status of soldiers based at the Castillo.

Dow Museum of Historic Houses★

149 Cordova St., St. Augustine. Open year-round Tue–Sat 10am–4:30pm; Sun 11am–4:30pm. $8.95. 904-823-9722. www.moas.org/dowmuseum.

Nine historic houses occupy a city block that was part of the original 16C walled colonial town. The oldest is the pink **Prince Murat House** (1790); the most recent is the **William Dean Howells House** (1910). Exhibits in **Star General Store** and other houses pertain to the French in Florida's history.

Government House Museum★

48 King St., St. Augustine. Open year-round daily 10am–4pm. $4. 904-825-5079. www.staugustine government.com.

The first construction on this site in 1599 included the governor's residence. A crumbling hulk by 1687, it was rebuilt of durable coquina but succumbed to fire during the British attack in 1702. Rebuilt by 1713, the house contains displays covering five centuries of St. Augustine's history.

Timucuan Ecological and Historic National Preserve★

13165 Mount Pleasant Rd., Jacksonville. Open year-round daily 9am–5pm. 904-641-7155. www.nps.gov/timu.

This 46,000-acre preserve, mostly salt marsh, interprets the area's cultural and natural history. Start at the **visitor center**, which has exhibits on the Timucua Indians, European exploration and the environment. Also on the grounds of the preserve, the **Fort Caroline National Memorial★** is a 1964 reproduction of a fort built by French Huguenot settlers on the south bank of the St. Johns River in the 1560s.

ANIMAL PARKS

St. Augustine Alligator Farm Zoological Park★

999 Anastasia Blvd., St. Augustine. Open year-round daily 9am–5pm. $21.95 ($10.95child 3-11). 904-824-3337. www.alligatorfarm.us.

Still waiting to see a Florida gator? Some 2,500 crocodilians live here in landscaped habitats and re-created swamps. The biggest is **Maximo**, a 15ft, 1,250-pound saltwater crocodile. **Land of Crocodiles** is Alligator Farm's outstanding collection of all 23 species of crocodilians. If you're feeling brave, try **Crocodile Crossing**, which lets you "zip" over the swamps – and gators! – on a zip line connecting some 50 platforms across 7 acres.

Jacksonville Zoo

370 Zoo Pkwy., Jacksonville. Open year-round daily 9am–5pm. $13.95, $8.95 child 3-12). 904-757-4463. www.jaxzoo.org.

With a menagerie of 1,800 exotic reptiles, birds and mammals and 1,000 varieties of plants thriving on its 120-acre site, this zoo ranks as a leader in botanical and zoological conservation. A highlight is the **African veldt**, where a boardwalk crosses a 16-acre grassy enclosure, home to lions, ostriches and gazelles. On the **Range of the Jaguar**, the big cats roam on 40 acres. Other exhibits bring you eye to eye with giraffes, gorillas, and some of the most venomous snakes in the world.

BEACHES

Amelia Island★★

42mi northeast of Jacksonville via A1A.

Virgin beaches, salt marshes and hardwood forests attract nature lovers to 13.5mi-long Amelia Island—one of the famous **Sea Islands**—while golf, tennis and high-end resorts lure luxury lovers. Be sure to stroll through the Centre Street Historic District in **Fernandina Beach★** to see the Victorian architecture.

Anastasia State Park

1340-A State Road A1A, St. Augustine. Open daily 8am–sunset. $8/car. 904-461-2033. www.floridastateparks.org/anastasia.

Devotees of sun and sand flock to the broad, lovely **beach★★** edging this 1,492-acre state park for some of the area's finest fishing, swimming and sunning. A protected saltwater lagoon provides excellent canoeing and windsurfing.

Kathryn Abbey Hanna Park

500 Wonderwood Dr., south of Mayport Naval Station, Jacksonville

A distinctly sylvan atmosphere lures visitors to this 450-acre oceanfront park, which boasts a splendid white-sand beach, hiking and biking trails, and a campground.

THE GREAT OUTDOORS

Cracker Creek Canoeing★

1795 Taylor Rd., W. Port Orange (southwest of Daytona Beach). Two-person canoes or kayaks $20/ hr or $50/day. 386-304-0788. www.oldfloridapioneer.com.

Paddle down Spruce Creek, a meandering blackwater stream that reveals an unspoiled landscape of cypress swamp and hardwood forest, and, maybe, a gator or two. Narrated pontoon boat tours (*Fri–Sun, 11am & 2pm; $10*) are also offered.

Kayak Amelia

13030 Heckscher Dr., Jacksonville. 904-251-0016. www.kayakamelia.com.

Kayak Amelia leads eco tours by kayak, bike, canoe or stand-up paddleboard from Amelia Island to St. Augustine. All kayak tours welcome beginners and start with a basic paddling lesson; tours average three hours and include a break for a snack and a swim. Guides are well-versed in the local salt marsh ecology.

Kayaking on Amelia Island

© Amelia Island Tourist Development Council

PERFORMING ARTS

The variety of performing arts, from local theater groups to nationally acclaimed musicians, on the Northeast Coast may surprise you.

First Coast Opera

Various venues, St. Augustine. 904-417-5555. www.firstcoast opera.com.

Now in its second decade of offering professional performances of opera and caberet theater, the First Coast Opera includes the likes of *The Barber of Seville, La Boheme,* and *The Threepenny Opera* in its impressive repertoire.

Florida Theatre

128 E. Forsyth St., Jacksonville. 904-355-2787. www.florida theater.com.

Beautifully restored as an attractive anchor on the St. Johns River, this vibrant venue offers more than 200 cultural and entertainment events annually from ballet and opera to contemporary pop, jazz and rock.

Limelight Theater
11 Old Mission Ave., St. Augustine.
904-825-1164 or 866-682-6400.
www.limelight-theatre.org.
Touted as one of North Florida's
top cultural organizations,
Limelight Theatre offers a broad
range of live performances in its
intimate 125-seat venue.

St. Augustine Amphitheater
1340 A1A South, St. Augustine.
904-471-1965. www.staug
amphitheatre.com.
Originally the home of Florida's
state play, the *Cross and the Sword*,
the amphitheater was refurbished
in 2002 as a venue for a variety of
performances and an audience
capacity of 4,100.

Times Union Center for Performing Arts
300 W. Water St., Jacksonville. 904-
633-6110. www.jaxevents.com/
timesunion.php.
A wide range of events is offered
year-round in three venues
here: The 1,800-seat Robert E.
Jacoby Symphony Hall, home to
the **Jacksonville Symphony
Orchestra**; the 3,000-seat Jim
and Jan Moran Theater for larger
events; and the 600-seat C. Herman
and Mary Virginia Terry Theater for
more intimate productions.

SHOPPING

**Just as Northeast Florida offered the first Spanish explorers a taste of
the exotic, modern shoppers can discover new retail territory here.**

The Avenues
10300 Southside Blvd.,
Jacksonville. Mon–Sat 10am–9pm,
Sun noon–6pm. 904-363-3054.
www.simon.com/mall/?id=124.
Anchors include Belk and Dillard's,
plus more than 150 of America's
favorite shopping destinations for
all ages and lifestyles.

Avonlea Antique Mall
8101 Philips Hwy., Jacksonville. Mon
–Sat 10am–6pm, Sun noon–6pm.
904-636-8785. www.avonlemall.com
More than 150 dealers in this
40,000sq-ft mall feature an array of
antiques, jewelry and collectibles.

Jacksonville Landing
2 W. Independent Dr.,
Jacksonville. Mon–Sat 10am–
8pm, Sun noon–5:30pm.
www.jacksonvillelanding.com.

On the downtown riverfront, this
mix of local and national retailers
has it all – from handcrafted
jewelry at AlyCat to the custom-
made fashions of Kara Bazma.

Lightner Antique Mall
25 Granada St., St Augustine.
Mon–Sun 11 am–4:30pm.
904-824-9948.
Adjacent to the Lightner Museum,
the mall comprises seven owner-
operated shops filled with a
treasure trove of antiques.

Shops of Historic Avondale
3562 St. Johns Ave., Jacksonville.
Mon–Sat 10 am–5pm.
www.shoppesofavondale.com.
Find more than 60 local businesses
with wares from Oriental rugs
to pet supplies in this unique
neighborhood setting.

MUST DO NORTHEAST COAST

St. Augustine Premium Outlets
2700 State Rd. 16, St. Augustine.
Mon–Sat, 9am–9pm, Sun 10am–
6pm. 904-825-1555.
www.premiumoutlets.com.
This is That Place. The one you can
count on to fulfill your shopaholic
urges with the best name-brands.

St. George Street
St. George between Orange and
Hypolita Sts., St. Augustine.
Browsing is a must-do along this
historic stem, which combines a
colonial atmosphere with world
class merchandise in a pedestrian-
only urban setting.

SPAS

**Something about the combination of sun, sand, and a resort
atmosphere brings out the desire to be pampered at one of the
area's many spas.**

Ponte Vedra Spa
200 Ponte Vedra Blvd., Ponte
Vedra Beach. 904-285-1111.
www.pontevedra.com.
A garden patio with a waterfall and
outdoor Jacuzzi, an oceanfront
gym and 22 treatment rooms
number among the inn's amenities.

Ritz-Carlton Spa
4750 Amelia Island Pkwy.,
Amelia Island. 904-277-1100.
www.ritzcarlton.com.
Paraffin hand and foot treatments,
a warm oil scalp massage and a
shea-butter body massage make
up the Ritz's signature Honey
Butter Wrap. Couples can revel in a
honey-vanilla milk bath.

The Spa at Omni Amelia
Island Plantation
6800 First Coast Hwy., Amelia
Island. 904-432-2220 or 877-843-
7722. www.spaamelia.com.
Complete spa services available to
Plantation guests and the public
include a variety of massage, yoga
and body treatments.

Spa at One Ocean
One Ocean Blvd., Atlantic
Beach. 904-249-7402.
www.oneoceanresort.com.
Combining a massage with a
soothing Hylunia facial, the
marine-inspired Ocean Breeze
Refresher echoes the spa's
oceanfront setting.

Northeast Coast Nightlife
Miami Beach has the reputation for glamour, the Keys get points for being
cool, but the Northeast Coast is satisfied with its own brand of good times.
Jacksonville has new energy with clubs such as **Mark's Downtown** (*315 E.
Bay St.; 904-355-509; www.marksjax.com*); **Tera Nova** (*8206 Phillips Hwy.; 800-
557-5808; teranovalounge.com*); and **Suite** (*4880 Big Island Dr.; 904-493-9305;
suitejacksonville.com*). Summer in Jax Beach brings an evening **jazz series**
that attracts regional and national artists.
In St. Augustine, **A1A Ale Works Brewery** (*1 King St.; 904-829-2977; www.a1a
aleworks.com*) offers fine brews and a view of Matanzas Bay, while the **Amelia
Island Museum of History** combines happy hour with history during the
Fernandina Pub Crawl Tour (*Thu; reservations: 904-261-7378 x105*).

ORLANDO AREA

The most popular tourist destination in the world, the Orlando area in central Florida attracts some 50 million visitors annually. Best known as the home of **Walt Disney World★★★**, the region also boasts the other "super-theme parks" of **Universal Studios★★★** and **SeaWorld★★★** as well as many other major visitor attractions. The city of Orlando itself, now the state's largest inland city, serves as the region's hub. Though mega-highways lined with chain hotels and shopping malls now web the flat, lake-pocked subtropical landscape, historic neighborhoods still grace the older parts of nearby cities and towns like **Kissimmee**, a placid residential community spreading along the shores of Lake Tohopekaliga about 10mi south of downtown Orlando. It's now known as "the Gateway to Disney" but still sports a charming downtown strip (Broadway) as well as a few low-key attractions, like **Gatorland★** *(407-855-5496; gatorland.com)*, an old-fashioned park with a newfangled zip line that lets you fly over the gator-filled swamp; and Green Meadows Farm *(407-846-0770; www.greenmeadowsfarm.com)*, a 40-acre farm where you can milk a cow, feed a goat, and (try to) catch a chicken.

Practical Information

When to Go

Daytime **temperatures** in Orlando average 61F/16C in January, 72F/22C in April, 83F/29C in July, and 74F/23C in October. The **theme parks** are most crowded during the Christmas holiday season, spring break and summer vacation, as well as on holidays like Halloween.

Getting There and Around

♦ **Orlando International Airport (MCO)** *(www.orlandoairports.net)* lies 7mi south of city and has all the major rental-car agencies.

♦ **Mears Transportation Group** offers 24hr **limos** *($125)*, **taxis** *($30–$35)* and **shuttle** vans *($17)* to downtown *(407-423-5566; www.mearstransportation.com)*.

♦ The Orlando Amtrak **train** station is at 1400 Sligh Blvd. *(800-872-7245; www.amtrak.com)*.

♦ Lynx provides the **local bus service** and is surprisingly wide-ranging and efficient *(year-round daily; $1; transfers 10¢; 407-841-2279; www.golynx.com)*.

♦ The I-Ride **trolley system** services the International Drive area *(daily 8am–10:30pm; every 20–30min; $1.25 per ride; all-day $4; 866-243-7483; www.iridetrolley.com)*.

Visitor Information

Stop by the **Official Visitor Center** at 8723 International Dr., Suite 101 *(open year-round daily 8:30am–6:30pm; 407-363-5872; www.visit orlando.com)* for trip-planning advice and the free **Orlando Magicard**, offering discounts on accommodations, attractions, dining and shopping. You can also get a Magicard through the website.

CITIES

ORLANDO★★★

Once a sleepy orange-producing area, sprawling metropolitan Orlando now ranks as one of the nation's fastest-growing cities, as well as one of the world's most popular tourist destinations.

Orlando Downtown Historic District

The eight-square-block core centering on **Orange Avenue★** has evolved into a lively nightspot for both residents and visitors, with a number of good restaurants and clubs. Drop by the **Orange County Regional History Center★** *(65 E. Central Blvd; 407-836-8500; www. thehistorycenter.org)* to get the skinny on what Central Florida was like before the advent of Disney.

Loch Haven Park

About a mile north of the downtown core, this 45-acre park is nestled between three lakes and holds Orlando's major museums.

The Orlando Museum of Art★ *(407-896-4231; www.omart.org)* focuses on American art, African art and art of the Americas.

The Orlando Science Center★ *(407-514-2000; www.osc.org)* has exhibits on topics from astronomy to dinosaurs, along with two theaters and an observatory.

The lakeside **Mennello Museum of American Folk Art** *(407-246-4278; www.mennellomuseum.com)* features works by Maine-born artist **Earl Cunningham** (1893–1977), who painted in St. Augustine for decades.

THEME PARKS

SEAWORLD ORLANDO★★★

7007 SeaWorld Dr. Open year-round daily 9am. Closing times vary. $80 ($72/child 3-9yrs). 407-351-3600 or 800-432-2424. www.seaworld.com.

This 200-acre marine adventure park mixes entertainment and education in its many animal shows, theme rides, touch pools and aquariums. The park is one of three SeaWorlds nationwide, which together support the world's largest collection of marine life. In addition to its public attractions, SeaWorld actively pursues research and breeding programs and assists wild animals in distress.

Animal Attractions

Key West at SeaWorld

This quirky village re-creates the spirit of Florida's farthest resort outpost. Attractions include **Stingray Lagoon**, where visitors can touch the broad flat fish as it swims by; **Turtle Point**, which introduces several endangered species; and **Dolphin Cove**, where staff members are on hand to stage playful interactions with the marine mammals.

Shark Encounter, SeaWorld Orlando
© SeaWorld Parks & Entertainment

Touring Tip

Plan your visit around scheduled show times; you can pick up a schedule at the front gate. Arrive early to get a good seat. For a bird's-eye view of the park, take a ride on the **Sky Tower**, which lifts passengers 400ft in a rotating chamber.

Manatee Rescue

This exhibit immerses visitors in the underwater world of the famed Florida manatee. You can watch these marine giants, some weighing 1,000 pounds, from above the water and below.

Pacific Point Preserve

Rocky shoals of an open-air pool capture the atmosphere of the Pacific coast. Harbor and fur seals bob in the waters, sea lions lounge on rocks, and a symphony of sounds is always in progress.

Penguin Encounter

Six thousand pounds of snow fall daily inside this frosty habitat, re-creating the Antarctic's rocky cliffs and frigid waters. Guests ride a 120ft-long moving walkway through the frozen wonderland to watch 200 of the playful birds cavort above and under the water.

Shark Encounter

At the entrance to this exhibit, a small outdoor pool houses of sharks and rays. Inside, visitors walk through an acrylic archway that tunnels through a 660,000-gallon aquarium with five species of sharks.

Thrill Rides

Journey to Atlantis
You are guaranteed to get wet—very wet—on this thrill ride, where a high-speed roller coaster carries you through dark passageways haunted by evil sirens, down a nearly vertical 60ft waterfall and around a pair of S-curves into another free-falling plunge as you search for the lost city of Atlantis. Not in the mood for a soaking? Check out the peaceful **Jewel of the Sea Aquarium** here instead.

Kraken
SeaWorld's wildest roller-coaster ride is floorless and billed as Orlando's "longest, fastest, tallest and steepest." If you have the stomach for it, you'll be whisked to the height of a 15-story building, plunged down at speeds of 65mph and turned upside-down seven times.

Manta
The newest ride is one of Orlando's finest, with a head-first, face-down twist, dipping into the water. Themed to resemble a flying manta ray, Manta is said to be the first "flying" roller coaster of its kind in the world.

Wild Arctic
A virtual-reality helicopter ride takes passengers pitching and rolling over a crevassed landscape above caribou, polar bears and narwhals. After narrowly escaping an avalanche, you'll disembark at a mock-up of an Arctic research station featuring above- and below-water views of beluga whales, walruses and harbor seals.

Shows
Additional shows are presented on a seasonal basis. See box office or website for details.

A'Lure: The Call of the Ocean
Tumblers, aerial artists and yo-yo artists star in this retelling of the Greek Sirens myth.

Blue Horizons
Dolphins and false killer whales star in this spectacle, along with a rainbow of exotic birds and a cast of world-class divers and aerialists draped in elaborate costumes.

Clyde and Seamore Take Pirate Island
A swashbuckling misadventure on the high seas stars the parks hilarious sea lions, otters and walruses.

One Ocean
SeaWorld's newest and most popular show stars the renowned five-ton killer whale Shamu, along with his protégés. Guided by their trainers, the whales leap and twirl to music amid dancing fountains. (If you sit up close, you're sure to get soaked.)

Pets Ahoy
Four-legged creatures, including dogs, cats, rats, skunks and potbellied pigs—many rescued from animal shelters—do all sorts of zany tricks in this silly show.

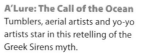

Touring Tip

As with all the theme parks, you'll get the best deal on **tickets** to **SeaWorld** by purchasing them online in advance.

THEME PARKS

UNIVERSAL ORLANDO★★★

1000 Universal Studios Plaza. Open year-round daily; hours vary by season. Site comprises both Universal Studios and Islands of Adventure. One park, one day: $82 ($74/child 3-9yrs); two parks, two days: $115 ($102/child). Other combination tickets available. 407-363-8000. www.universal orlando.com.

Shrek 4-D, Universal Orlando

At close to 840 acres, techno-savvy **Universal Orlando** gives Disney a run for its money. Indeed, many people (teens in particular) prefer this park to the Mouse's offering. Initially a single theme park and working movie studio, it now includes a second theme park, **Islands of Adventure**, plus **Universal CityWalk**, a massive dining, entertainment and shopping complex. Also linked to the parks are several resort hotels.

Universal Studios Florida

Universal Studios Florida—the original 444-acre theme park and working studio, opened in 1990—ranks as the largest motion-picture and television facility outside Hollywood. Intended as a place where visitors can "ride the movies," the park bases its attractions on popular films and television shows. There are also two outdoor play areas.

Thrill Rides

Ten thrill rides in the park pull out all the stops to shock and amaze, blitzing and shaking you into a state of stupefied satisfaction. Opened in 2009, **Hollywood Rip Ride Rockit** is Orlando's tallest roller coaster at 17 stories. After you pick your own rock music soundtrack, you'll be subjected to heart-stopping elements, including the world's first non-inverting loop. On the other end of the spectrum, **Woody Woodpecker's Nuthouse Coaster** is gentle enough for toddlers, gliding through the maniacally laughing bird's nut factory.

Most of the other rides are based on blockbuster movies. **Disaster!** was originally based on the 1974 flick *Earthquake* but was remade in 2007 as a roundup of disaster movies, starring Christopher Walken and the city of San Francisco. Other thrillers include **E.T. Adventure; Jaws; Men in Black Alien Attack; Revenge of the Mummy; Shrek 4-D;** and **Twister: Ride It Out**.

Shows

Combining live action and video, Universal Studios' seven shows cater to all ages: **A Day in the Park with Barney** is geared for tots, while **Lucy: A Tribute** (to Lucille Ball), will appeal to grandparents. For everyone in between, there's **Fear Factor Live**, an "extreme" audience participation show; **Beetlejuice's Graveyard Revue**, a live stage show; and others.

Attractions

Universal's Islands of Adventure

Opened in 1999, this is one of the most technologically advanced and imaginative theme parks you'll experience anywhere. Seven themed "islands" are grouped around a large lagoon. Each has restaurants, several live shows, and four sport play areas. **Port of Entry** serves as a shopping and dining area as well as a departure point.

Jurassic Park

On **River Adventure**, the premier ride here, you'll suddenly find yourself in the Raptor Containment Area, surrounded by meat-eating dinosaurs. The only escape from the terrifying *Tyrannosaurus rex* is down an 85ft water chute.

The Lost Continent

Come here to see two live shows: **Poseidon's Fury**, prominently featuring lasers and flames, and the the stunt-filled **Eighth Voyage of Sinbad**.

Marvel Super Hero Island

Doctor Doom's Fearfall rockets you 150ft into the air, then plunges you back to earth even faster. Don a pair of 3-D night-vision goggles on the **Amazing Adventures of**

Spider-Man, filled with speed and special effects. A series of chilling swoops and loops define the classic **Incredible Hulk Coaster**.

Seuss Landing

This whimsical island features the characters of author Theodor "Dr. Seuss" Geisel, with a carousel, a **Cat in the Hat** ride, and a cafe that serves green eggs and ham.

Toon Lagoon

Classic cartoon characters come to life in the Pandemonium Cartoon Circus and two water rides: Dudley Do-Right's Ripsaw Falls and Popeye and Bluto's Bilge-Rat Barges.

🚂 Wizarding World of Harry Potter

Opened in 2010, this fabulously popular "park within a park" occupies 20 acres. Here you'll find an awesome re-creation of Hogwarts School as well as two roller coasters: **Dragon Challenge** comprises two dueling high-speed coasters, while **Flight of the Hippogriff** is a gentler ride that's appropriate for little ones. **Harry Potter and the Forbidden Journey** is a state-of-the-art adventure that starts at the Hogwarts School before soaring above the castle and coming face to face with magical creatures.

Touring Tip

Arrive 30min to 1hr prior to opening time. As soon as the gates open, head for **Hollywood Rip Ride Rockit** or to **The Wizarding World of Harry Potter**, the park's most popular attractions. Visit less high-profile rides and shows in the middle of the day, when other lines are likely to be the longest. You can bypass the lines by spending $20-$70 more per person for an Express Pass or staying at one of the onsite hotels, which include passes (along with early admission to Harry Potter) in the room rate.

WALT DISNEY WORLD RESORT★★★

3111 World Dr., Lake Buena Vista (Magic Kingdom). Opening and closing times vary by day and season. Theme park tickets start at $82 for one day ($74/child 3-9yrs), dropping to $35.29/$32 per day if you stay for a week. Many package deals are available. 407-939-1289. disneyworld.disney.go.com.

This mega-size theme park and resort is the top vacation destination resort on the planet. Truly a world unto itself, the immense 29,900-acre (47sq mi) complex—about twice the size of Manhattan—lies 20 miles southwest of downtown Orlando and encompasses four theme parks (Magic Kingdom, Epcot, Disney's Animal Kingdom and Disney's Hollywood Studios),

more than 20 resort hotels, eight nightclubs, two water parks, five golf courses, a sports complex, numerous lakes, a zoo and more.

🏰 Magic Kingdom★★★

The 107-acre park has six areas that radiate out from Cinderella Castle. This is the most child-friendly of all the theme parks, so if you have little ones in tow, start here. Check the park brochure for a schedule of the day's shows and special events. Below are highlights of each section.

Adventureland

Little ones love the **Magic Carpets of Aladdin** ride, while everyone wants to climb aboard a boat to experience the **Pirates of the Caribbean** ride, which still embodies the spirit of Disney at its best.

ORLANDO, UNIVERSAL ORLANDO ↗

Map of the Walt Disney World Resort area showing: Lake Tibet Butler, Sand Lake Rd. 439 482, Winter Garden, Doctor Phillips, Lake Mable, Lake Sheen, Apopka, Big Sandy Lake, 528, International Dr., MAGIC KINGDOM, Bay Lake, Vineland 535, Pocket Lake, Reedy Lake, Floridian, Monorail, SEAWORLD ORLANDO, Vineland, Walt Disney Speedway, WALT DISNEY WORLD RESORT, EPCOT Center, Western Way, World Dr., Buena Vista Blvd. 535, 4, Buena Vista Dr., Lake Bryan, EPCOT, L. Buena Vista, Dr., International Dr., DISNEY'S ANIMAL KINGDOM, Buena Dr., Lake Cecile 192, DISNEY'S HOLLYWOOD STUDIOS, Orange County, 536, 417, Osceola County, 192 Blizzard Beach, Irlo Bronson, Mem. Hwy., 417 Pkwy., N. Poinciana Blvd., Sand Hill Rd., 545, 4, Celebration, Osceola

Scale: 0–2 mi / 0–3 km, N

BEE LINE EXPWY ↗ KENNEDY SPACE CENTER →

TAMPA BAY AREA ↙   KISSIMMEE ↘

Fantasyland

With its fairy-tale atmosphere, this area captivates anyone who has seen the Disney classics. The icon of the park, **Cinderella Castle**, is a Gothic extravaganza. The most famous (and schmaltzy) ride within the Magic Kingdom is **It's a Small World**, a boat trip past 500 Audio-Animatronic® children and animals representing nearly 100 nations, all singing the repetitive theme song.

Frontierland

At **Country Bear Jamboree**, a winsome troupe of Audio-Animatronic® "Bear-itones" delight crowds with their down-home performances.
If you want to cool off, board a dugout for a languid float and drenching dive at **Splash Mountain**.

Liberty Square

A celebration of old-time America, Liberty Square is home to a replica **White House**, populated by Audio-Animatronic® presidents; a **Haunted Mansion**; and the three-decker, gingerbread-trimmed **Liberty Belle** riverboat.

Main Street, U.S.A.

Tidy Victorian storefronts re-create an early-19C town ambience here. Cartoon-character-filled **parades** and **street parties** are common every afternoon, as are **fireworks** at night.

Tomorrowland

There's no doubting the favorite here: the **Space Mountain** roller coaster. Not for the faint of heart, a train hurtles passengers through near-darkness, plunging them into sudden, atmospheric comet showers and past twinkling stars.

Epcot★★★

Open year-round daily from 9am (World Showcase open 11am). Closing times vary.

More than two and a half times the size of the Magic Kingdom at 300 acres, Epcot (short for Experimental Prototype Community of Tomorrow) is divided into two distinct areas: Future World and World Showcase.

Future World

The iconic geodesic sphere **Spaceship Earth** stands at the entrance to Epcot. Inside, visitors

Dawn of Disney

In 1965, having secretly purchased almost 30,000 acres in Orange and Osceola counties, **Walt Disney**, the animated-film wizard and creator of California's Disneyland, announced plans to build a theme park outside Orlando. Overnight, land values in the area skyrocketed; throughout the rest of the decade, development engulfed the communities to the southwest along the I-4 corridor. Walt Disney World opened to great fanfare in 1971. SeaWorld followed two years later, and Universal Studios Florida joined the local theme-park ranks in 1990. In the intervening years, metropolitan Orlando tripled its population and now boasts the largest concentration of hotel rooms in the US. With some 50 million visitors annually, the area now ranks as one of the top commercial tourist destinations in the world.

THEME PARKS

Spaceship Earth, EPCOT

© Disney

- ◆ **Mission: SPACE** - Hop aboard a Mars flight simulator.
- ◆ **The Seas with Nemo and Friends** - Tunnel through the world's largest man-made saltwater aquarium and see a sea-turtle show.
- ◆ **Test Track** - Buckle up and feel what experimental cars endure, including road handling, impact-testing and suspension checks.
- ◆ **Universe of Energy** In this solar-powered pavilion, comedian Ellen DeGeneres takes a trip back to the Big Bang to learn the origin of fossil fuels.

spiral up 18 stories in a "time machine" past animated scenes depicting the history of human communication from prehistoric tribes to the present. The ground floor has interactive exhibits.

Elsewhere in Future World:
- ◆ **Imagination!** - Come see the 3D movie musical **Captain EO**, starring Michael Jackson, and try your hand at conducting an orchestra and making a video.
- ◆ **Innoventions** - The hands-on play space in two buildings teaches lessons on financial planning, fire and product safety, and the environment
- ◆ **The Land** - Take a boat ride through a simulated rain forest, desert and prairie before emerging into the pavilion's greenhouse gardens, where scientists work to perfect growing methods. The IMAX presentation **Soarin'** sends you on a peaceful hang-gliding flight over California.

World Showcase
The 1.3mi promenade at World Showcase circles a 40-acre lagoon and passes the pavilions of 11 countries. Each pavilion—staffed by nationals of the country it represents—reflects the authentic architecture, foods, crafts, costumes and traditions of that culture.

Live performers are often on hand to play music or demonstrate other artistic endeavors specific to their native land. Some pavilions also feature rides or large-scale films, museum-quality artifacts, and, most important, excellent restaurants.

Live stage shows are held at **America Gardens Theatre**. In the evenings, the World Showcase lagoon and pavilions become the setting for **IllumiNations**, an extravaganza of laser lights, music, fountains and fireworks.

Disney's Animal Kingdom★★★

Open year-round daily, usually 9am to 7pm.

Disney's newest theme park is home to some 1,700 animals (of 250 species) and four million plants (of 3,000 species)—as well as countless fantastical creatures, this being Disney—on more than 500 acres of land.

Asia and Africa

🦁 **Kilimanjaro Safaris** are the leading attraction of the Africa section. Open-sided all-terrain trucks carry passengers to the Serengeti Plain to look for rhinoceroses, elephants, lions, cheetahs, zebras, giraffes, baboons, gazelles and antelopes, and other residents of the savanna.
In Asia, the **Kali River Rapids** is a whitewater splash fest through foaming rapids. The most popular ride is the **Expedition Everest**, a high-speed roller coaster.
In **DinoLand U.S.A.**, a 12-passenger "Time Rover" takes you back to late-Cretaceous times to bring home a living dinosaur . . . just before an asteroid strikes the planet.

Kilimanjaro Safaris, Disney's Animal Kingdom
© Disney

Discovery Island

This is the giant, intricately carved **Tree of Life**. Beneath the "roots" of the tree, **It's Tough to Be a Bug!** is an 8min 3D multimedia show with termite sneezes (you'll get wet), a cloud of pesticide (simulated fog), and even a gentle sting! At **Camp Minnie-Mickey** younger children can interact with favorite Disney characters and see the splashy show **Festival of the Lion King**.

Disney's Hollywood Studios★★★

Open year-round daily at 9am. Closing times vary.

This relatively compact theme park celebrates the magic of filmmaking, from animation and stuntsmanship to adventure and romance. Art Deco architecture throughout the 154-acre site re-creates the Hollywood of the 1930s and 40s.
As always, get there before the official opening time and as soon as you get in, head for the most popular sights, in this case The **Twilight Zone™ Tower of Terror** and **Rock 'n' Roller Coaster Starring Aerosmith**—both stomach-churning thrill rides—and the **American Idol Experience**, which stars visitors to the park in a live re-creation of the smash-hit TV show.
Budding auteurs will love the behind-the-scenes **Studio Backlot Tour** and **The Magic of Disney Animation** show, and for George Lucas mavens there's the recently refurbished **Star Tours** ride.
Live performers make a splash in a number of live shows, including **Beauty and the Beast**; and on select nights, stick around for the laser show **Fantasmic!**

THEME PARKS

EXCURSION

Kennedy Space Center★★★

In the town of Orsino, 45min east of Orlando by car. Visitor complex open year-round daily 9am–6pm. Bus tours (2hr) depart every 15min beginning at 10am; last tour 2:45 pm. Closed Dec 25 and some launch days. $43 ($33/child 3-11yrs) includes all exhibits, IMAX films, bus tour and Astronaut Hall of Fame. Special interest tours cost an additional $21 each. 321-449-4444. www.kennedyspacecenter.com.

Three, two, one—blast off! Protruding from Florida's Atlantic coast, this barrier island of orange groves, tidal flats and pristine beaches is home to the nation's space program. Every US rocket—from the one that carried the Explorer I satellite in 1958 to the space shuttles launched to visit the International Space Station—has blasted off from Merritt Island or adjoining Cape Canaveral.

Visitor Complex

There's a lot to do here for adults and kids alike. The **Astronaut Encounter** is a meet-and-greet with a veteran astronaut. The **Shuttle Launch Experience** lets you board a space shuttle and feel what it's like to take off. **Exploration Space: Explorers Wanted** is a live-action interactive show. There are also exhibits on **Robotic Probes** and **Early Space Exploration**. The **Rocket Garden** displays impressive interstellar hardware, while the **Astronaut Memorial** pays tribute to fallen heroes of the space program. In the **Children's Play Dome,** little ones can burn off some steam:

IMAX films

Projected on screens more than five stories high, two IMAX films—*Hubble 3D* and *Space Station 3D,* narrated by Leonardo DiCaprio and Tom Cruise, respectively—include stunning footage shot from space. Seat-rumbling, six-channel digital stereo adds to the realistic effect.

Bus Tour

The 2hr narrated bus tour is a must. See the gigantic cubic **Vehicle Assembly Building**, where the shuttle is assembled (and where the *Apollo* and many other craft were built). At **Launch Complex 39**, visitors can climb a 60ft observation gantry and, perhaps, see a shuttle awaiting launch from another nearby complex. An excellent movie about the *Apollo 11* mission and a close-up inspection of a Saturn V moon rocket highlight a stop at the **Apollo/Saturn V Center.** Tours of the **Launch Control Center** include a stirring multimedia review of the Apollo series and displays of original lunar-excursion and command-service modules.

Kennedy Space Center

Courtesy Kennedy Space Center

ORLANDO AREA

MUST SEE

THE GREAT OUTDOORS

Bok Tower Gardens National Historic Landmark★★

1151 Tower Blvd., Lake Wales (35mi south of Kissimmee). Open year-round daily 8am–6pm (last admission 5pm). $10; $16 includes Pinewood Estate. 863-676-1408. boktowergardens.org.

Born in the Netherlands, publishing executive **Edward William Bok** (1863–1930) decided to create a nature sanctuary as a gift to the American people. He invited Frederick Law Olmsted Jr., son of the famed designer of New York City's Central Park, to transform a sandy, pine-covered site atop Iron Mountain into a botanical haven. The 130-acre park was dedicated in 1929 at ceremonies led by President Calvin Coolidge.

Gardens and Tower
Begin at the **visitor center** to view an introductory film and displays on the gardens' history. From here, wander along paths amid lush stands of live oaks, conifers, palm trees and ferns. Ever-changing splashes of color are painted seasonally on this green canvas by flowering plants, among them **azaleas** *(in bloom Dec–Mar)* and **camellias** *(Nov–Mar)*. Encircled by a placid moat, the 205ft Gothic Revival **tower** of Georgia marble and coquina is the focal point of the gardens. Its famous **carillon** of 57 bronze bells rings out every half hour and gives 45-minute concerts each day at 1pm and 3pm.

Pinewood Estate
Mon–Sat noon–4pm, Sun 1–4pm. The 20-room mansion, with its own lovely grounds, is considered one of the best examples of Mediterranean-style residential architecture in the state.

Harry P. Leu Gardens★

1920 N. Forest Ave., Orlando. Open year-round daily 9am–5pm. $7 (free first Mon of month). 407-246-2620. www.leugardens.org.

Orlando businessman and exotic-plant collector Harry P. Leu donated his house and 50-acre botanical reserve to the city in 1961. Situated along the southern shore of Lake Rowena, the gardens are renowned for their **camellias** *(in peak bloom Dec–mid-Feb)* and encompass the largest formal **rose garden** in the state *(in bloom Mar–Jan)*. Built as a farmhouse in 1888, the two-story, white-frame **Leu House Museum** is also open for tours *(daily 10am–3:30pm; closed July).*

The Orlando Magic

One of the National Basketball Association's most successful expansion teams, the **Orlando Magic** *(407-896-2442; www.nba.com/magic)* has made the playoffs 13 of its 22 years. As the only major professional sports team to play in Orlando, it has a major local following, with fans packing the new **Amway Center**, home of the league's largest Jumbotron.

PERFORMING ARTS

From Mick Jagger to Mickey Mouse, artists will find an appreciative audience in a variety of venues.

ORLANDO AREA

MUST DO

Amway Center
400 W. Church St., Orlando. 407-440-7000. www.amwaycenter.com.
Home of Orlando Magic NBA basketball and Orlando Predators AFL football, the 875,000sq ft arena features the largest high-definition scoreboard in an NBA venue. Performances by national entertainers and Broadway touring companies pack the house.

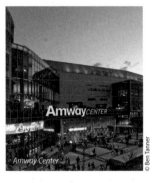

© Ben Tanner

Amway Center

Bob Carr Performing Arts Centre
401 W. Livingston St., Orlando. 407-849-2577. www.orlando venues.net.
Located in downtown Orlando and seating over 2,500, the Carr features excellent acoustics that make it ideal for concerts, Broadway shows, symphony orchestras, ballet and opera.

Florida Citrus Bowl Stadium
1610 W. Church St., Orlando. 407-849-2000. www.orlandovenues.net.
Seating over 70,000 patrons and currently undergoing a

$10-million facelift, Orlando's largest performance venue brings in both national bowl games and legendary performers.

Mad Cow Theatre
105 S. Magnolia Ave., Orlando. 407-297-8788. www.madcow theatre.com.
This professional theater company, established in 1997, stages both classic and contemporary drama. The group also sponsors the annual three-week Orlando Carbaret Festival.

Orlando Shakespeare Theater
812 E. Rollins St., Orlando. 407-447-1700. www.orlando shakes.org.
The Orlando Shakespeare Theater partners with the University of Central Florida to produce a full season of professional-quality theater, develop new plays, and provide educational experiences for the community.

UCF Arena
N. Gemini Blvd., Building 50, Orlando. 407-823-3070. www.ucfarena.com.
Located on the campus of the University of Central Florida, this entertainment and sports arena stages a diverse calendar, from top-name performers such as Katy Perry to Disney's *Phineas and Ferb*. The arena seats more than 10,000, with amenities that include luxury suites, loge boxes and club seating.

SHOPPING

With a vibrant downtown, nine major malls, and theme-park stores designed to please a princess, the Orlando area is a shopper's paradise.

Downtown Orlando

If a change of pace is what you're after, head downtown. Stroll the streets, window shop, and uncover unusual merchandise in shops such as **The Orange Avenue Antique Market** *(1829 N Orange Ave., Orlando; 407-895-9911);* and the **Urban Think Bookstore** *(625 E. Central Blvd.; 407-650-8004; www.urbanthinkorlando.com).*

Downtown Disney
1780 E. Buena Vista Dr., Lake Buena Vista. Call for hours. 407-828-3800. disneyworld.disney.go.com/destinations
This is ground zero for all things Disney. Here you can purchase stuffed cartoon characters, pins for trading, Tinkerbell T-shirts, and other mementos to make the magic last. Shops at Downtown Disney West Side and Pleasure Island sell everything from cigars to sunglasses.

Epcot Center
1200 Epcot Resort Blvd., Lake Buena Vista. Call for hours. 407-824-4321. disneyworld.disney.go.com/parks/epcot.
The Mouse Gear shop is the largest purveyor of Disney merchandise and apparel in Epcot; it's located in Innoventions Plaza behind Spaceship Earth in Future World.

The Mall at Millenia
4200 Conroy Rd., Orlando. Open Mon–Sat 10am–9pm, Sun 11am–7pm. www.mallatmillenia.com.
Located near the northern end of International Drive, the upscale mall claims the first and largest Macy's in central Florida. More than 150 specialty stores run the gamut from housewares at Crate & Barrel to oh-so-chic shoes at Jimmy Choo.

Orlando Premium Outlets
4200 Conroy Rd., Orlando. Open Mon–Sat 10am–9pm, Sun 11am–7pm. www.mallatmillenia.com.
Savings and style go hand in hand at the 150 upscale outlets here. Find bargains on a host of brand names encompassing Ann Taylor, Burberry, Coach, Elizabeth Arden, Giorgio Armani, Salvatore Ferragamo and many more.

Universal Studios CityWalk
6000 Universal Blvd., Orlando. Call for hours. 407-363-8000. universalorlando.com.
Merchandise related to your favorite Universal film characters abounds here, along with the latest in fashion and accessories.

© Leabrooks Photography / Alamy

The Mall at Millenia, Orlando

NIGHTLIFE

Unlike many cities where nightlife is a decidedly adult activity, Orlando's evening entertainment scene includes something for everyone in its ever-changing menu of excitement. Cover charges may apply for clubs.

Church Street
W. Church St., Orlando. 407-649-4270. www.churchstreetbars.com.
For the nightspot aficionado, Church Street is the heart of the action with bars like Latitudes, Big Belly and Chillers and Antigua making up the core of Orlando's party central.

Epcot Center
Lake Buena Vista. 407-824-4321. disneyworld.disney.go.com/parks/epcot.
IlumiNations: Reflections of Earth depicts the history of earth and its people with a dazzling display of pyrotechnics, music, fountains and special lighting effects. The 14-minute spectacle takes place at the World Showcase Lagoon. Check the Epcot park guide for show times.

Downtown Disney
1780 East Buena Vista Dr., Lake Buena Vista. 407-828-3800. disneyworld.disney.go.com/destinations/downtown-disney.
Downtown Disney West Side is the home of the House of Blues as well as movie theaters, the DisneyQuest indoor interactive theme park, and the hugely popular (and very expensive) Cirque du Soleil theater.
Pleasure Island, undergoing renovations in 2011, offers music performances and dancing for kids.

Pointe Orlando Universal's Islands of Adventure
9101 International Dr., Orlando. 407-355-7711. www.pointeorlando.com.
Not far from the theme parks, and across the street from the Orlando Convention and Visitors Bureau, Pointe Orlando is home to the rockin' BB King Blues Club; an IMAX movie theater; the Improv Comedy Club and Fat Fish Blue; and the Pointe Performing Arts Center.

Universal Studios
6000 Universal Blvd., Orlando. 407-363-8000. universalorlando.com.
After a day at the parks, unwind at **Universal CityWalk**, where you can enjoy a libation and listen to live music. Get your groove on at **Hard Rock Live** at the Coliseum of Rock and Roll, enjoy cocktails at the **Velvet Bar**, and sample the Hawaiian experience at **Wantilan Luau**. And that's just for starters!

Walt Disney World's Wishes Nighttime Spectacular
Main Street at Disney Magic Kingdom Theme Park, Lake Buena Vista. 407-939-3463. disneyworld.disney.go.com.
Regardless of age, gender, or belief in fairies, few people experience this extravaganza of fireworks, music and Disney magic without getting goosebumps. It's the perfect end to a day at Disney.

SPAS

Whether you're hobnobbing with cartoon characters, golfing, or late-night club-hopping, take time to luxuriate in the area's hotel spas.

Disney Spas

disneyworld.disney.go.com.
Walt Disney World in Lake Buena Vista offers three full-service spas open to the public as well as resort guests. **The Grand Floridian Spa** at Disney's Grand Floridian Resort & Spa *(4401 Floridian Way; 407-824-3000)* provides pampering for adults and children, in addition to a boutique and access to workout equipment. **The Spa at Disney's Saratoga Springs Resort & Spa** *(1960 Broadway; 407-827-1100)* doles out massage and body wraps in a setting reminiscent of early 20C upstate New York.
At **Mandara Spa** *(Swan & Dolphin Hotel, 1500 Epcot Resorts Blvd.; 407-934-4772)*, a Balinese vibe infuses the treatments.

Disney's Grand Floridian Spa

© Disney

Eo Inn & Spa

Eo Inn, 227 N. Eola Dr., Orlando. 407-481-8485 or toll-free 888-481-8488. www.eoinn.com/spa.
Among a wide array of services here, the Desert Heat Body Cocoon is a warm bubbling wrap stress-buster, and the Green Coffee Slimming Body Wrap targets cellulite. Pressed for time? The On The Go package abbreviates a facial, massage and pedicure.

Poseidon Spa

Grand Bohemian Hotel, 325 S. Orange Ave., Orlando. 407-313-9000 or toll-free 888-213-9110. www.grandbohemianhotel.com.
Moments from downtown and the theme parks, Poseidon Spa reflects the luxury of the Grand Bohemian brand. Pamper yourself with a the Jewels of the Sea body treatment or a heated shell massage.

The Spa at Shingle Creek

Rosen Shingle Creek Hotel, 9939 Universal Blvd., Orlando. 407-996-9772. www.spaatshinglecreek.com.
At this resort spa, the full menu of massage, body and skin treatments take on a Florida theme. Try an Everglades Scrub and Body Wrap or a Creekside Citrus and Cedar Massage, which employs the aromatherapy benefits of white cedar, spruce and lime oils.

The Waldorf Astoria Spa by Guerlain®

Waldorf Astoria Orlando, 14200 Bonnet Creek Resort Lane, Orlando. 407-597-5500. www.waldorfastoriaorlando.com.
Transforming treatments in the Waldorf's 22 luxurious rooms include aromatherapy and soothing massage as well as a host of day spa packages. After your treatment, relax in the steam room or soak in the Jacuzzi.

THE PANHANDLE

Sandwiched between Georgia, Alabama and the Gulf of Mexico, the Panhandle extends 200mi westward from the Florida peninsula in a band 30 to 100 miles wide. The region lies far enough north to have a summer tourist season and far enough west to be in a different time zone from the rest of Florida (Central Time Zone begins at the Apalachicola River, 45mi west of Tallahassee).

Spanish explorers gained an early toehold here in 1559, when Tristan de Luna established a short-lived settlement at Pensacola -- six years before the founding of St. Augustine. Spain failed to rediscover northwest Florida until the late 17 C, and jockeyed with France for control of Pensacola Bay for nearly half a century.

Today, the Panhandle's sparkling white-sand beaches, especially those in and around **Panama City Beach**, draw thousands of sun-seeking vacationers and retirees every year, and while it can seem that the coast is chock-a-block with resorts and other commercial development, the **Gulf Islands National Seashore**, along with a number of gorgeous state parks, protects large chunks of wild beach and dune environment. Snorkeling and sportfishing are both popular pastimes on the Gulf Coast, where you can also get your fill of local oysters. Inland you'll find rolling hills clad with pines and hardwoods, farms and—even in the state capital of **Tallahassee**—a culture that has more in common with its Deep South neighbors, Georgia and Alabama, than other parts of Florida.

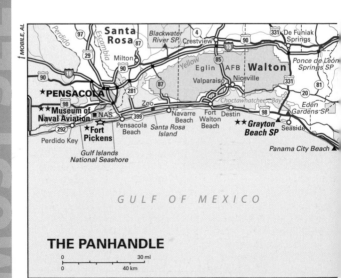

THE PANHANDLE

Practical Information

When to Go
If it's sunbathing and swimming you're looking for, visit in the summer or early fall. It can be humid inland, but Gulf breezes will keep you comfortable on the coast; daytime **temperatures** **average 83F/28C in Pensacola in July**. Spring and fall are also lovely times to see the region's beautiful state parks and historic neighborhoods..

Getting There by Air
* **Pensacola Gulf Coast Regional Airport (PNS)** serves the west end of the Panhandle (*800-436-5000; www.flypensacola.com*)

* **Tallahassee Regional Airport (TLF)** serves the east end (*850-891-7802; www.talgov.com/airport*). Both have major car-rental agencies; follow signs to ground transportation. Driving is definitely the easiest way to explore the region.

Visitor Information
All major towns in the Panhandle have a visitor information bureau, and some have walk-in centers (call or check websites for addresses and hours):
* **Apalachicola** – *850-653-9419; www.apalachicolabay.org.*
* **Panama City Beach** – *850-233-6503; www.visitpanamacitybeach.com.*
* **Pensacola** – *850-434-1234; www.visitpensacola.com.*
* **Tallahassee** – *850-606-2305; www.visittallahassee.com.*

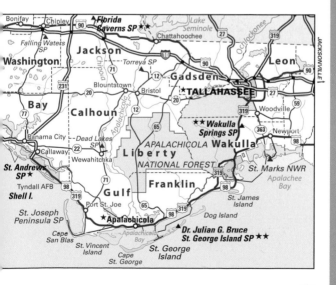

THE PANHANDLE

CITIES

APALACHICOLA★

Occupying the tip of a spit of land where the Apalachicola River empties into the Gulf of Mexico, Apalachicola (a Creek word meaning "land beyond") is a serene little fishing community of some 2,000 souls. Within the last two decades, tourists have discovered the excellent deep-sea fishing and laid-back lifestyle in this formerly isolated area. The Apalachicola basin boasts one of the country's largest **oyster nurseries**, producing more than three-fourths of Florida's annual crop. For a sampling, visit during the **Florida Seafood Festival** 🎣 *(early Nov; www.floridaseafoodfestival.com).* Walking-tour maps of the **historic downtown★** are available at the visitor center *(122 Commerce St.).* Spend an hour or so to see some of the town's lovely antebellum structures and atmospheric cemetery *(Chestnut St between 6th and 8th St. E.),* then drive to the stunning beach at **Dr. Julian G. Bruce St. George Island State Park★★** *(See Beaches).*

PENSACOLA★

Hugging the western shore of Pensacola Bay, **Pensacola** (pop. 54,055) sports three contiguous historic districts in its downtown core, making it a great city for exploring on foot.
South of downtown, the **Port of Pensacola** is the largest port of the Panhandle, while the **Naval Air Station Pensacola** is home to the vast **National Museum of Naval Aviation★★** *(See Museums).*

Seville Historic District★
Pick up a walking-tour map at the visitor center (1401 E. Gregory St.). Concentrated between Tarragona and Florida Blanca Streets and Garden and Main, Seville is the oldest of the three contiguous historic districts, brimming with frame vernacular, Victorian and Creole houses. Streets here were plotted by the British in 1765 and renamed by the Spanish.
Within this district is **Historic Pensacola Village**, made up of 27 properties, 11 of which are museums and homes *(Tue–Sat 10am–4pm; guided tours 11am, 1pm & 2.30pm; $6; 850-595-5988; www.historicpensacola.org).*

Palofax Historic District★
Along Palafox St. from Garden St. to Pine St.
Palafox Street, the commercial spine of Pensacola since the late 19C, retains the look of earlier days. Stroll the streets leading down to the water to see the 1907 Beaux-Arts **Blount Building**, the Spanish Baroque **Saenger Theatre** (1925), and the massive 1887 **Escambia County Courthouse**.
Overlooking **Plaza Ferdinand VII**, the **T.T. Wentworth Jr. Florida State Museum** is a massive cabinet of curiosities *(330 S. Jefferson St, open Tue–Sat 10am–4pm; $6; 850-595-5990; www.historicpensacola.org).*

TALLAHASSEE★

Set amid rolling hills some 12mi from the Georgia state line and 20mi from the Gulf of Mexico, Florida's capital city (pop. 243,870)

Canopy Roads★

Driving guide available at the visitor center. Shaded by an airy vault of moss-draped live oak, sweet gum and hickory branches, five specially designated historic roads fan out from Tallahassee. **Old St. Augustine Road** is the oldest of the routes, dating to the 1600s. It contains cool stretches of dense canopy from Capitol Circle to Williams Road. **Old Bainbridge Road** (*Route 361*) was originally a Native American trail. The canopied portion of **Meridian Road** (*Route 155*) is north of I-10. **Centerville Road** (*Route 151*) is canopied east of Capitol Circle. From there it winds along a shaded 17mi course, passing through the tiny community of Chemonie Crossing and ending at Miccosukee. Vast acres of plantation woodland still line picturesque **Miccosukee Road** (*Route 146*), where you'll also find the **Goodwood Museum & Gardens★** (*see Historic Sites*).

was considered a sleepy southern town until its development in the 1970s and 80s. Still, its moss-draped live oaks, azaleas and gracious old houses evoke an Old South charm, and the presence of Florida State University and Florida A&M gives it a youthful pulse.

Downtown

Pick up a walking-tour map at the visitor center (106 E. Jefferson St.). The heart of downtown Tallahassee is the **Capitol Complex★** (*400 S. Monroe St.*). Dating from 1845, the **Old Capitol★** has been a museum since 1982 (*Mon–Fri 9am–4:30pm, Sat 10am–4:30pm, Sun noon–4:30pm; 850-487-1902; www.fl historiccapitol.gov*). Step inside to see the **Old Supreme Court Chamber** and the former **House and Senate Chambers**. Next door, the 22-story **New Capitol** (1978) is the city's tallest building; its observation deck offers sweeping **views★** (*open business hours*). Lined with restaurants and offices, serpentine **Adams Street Commons** (*between Pensacola St. and College Ave.*) is a pleasant lunchtime retreat. On the other side of City Hall sits the **Mary Brogan Museum of Art and Science (MOAS)**, a Smithsonian affiliate with three floors of exhibits (*350 S. Duval St.; Mon–Sat 10am–5pm, Sun 1–5pm; $10; 850-513-0700; www.thebrogan.org*), and the **Challenger Learning Center of Tallahassee** (*425 W. Jefferson St.; 850-645-7796; www.challengertlh.com*), site of an IMAX theater and high-definition planetarium dome.

Park Avenue Historic District★
Park Ave. from Macomb St. to N. Meridian St.
Anchored on the west by the city's two oldest **cemeteries**, the district spreads eastward to the 1854 **Meginniss-Munroe House**, now home to the city's most esteemed local gallery, the **LeMoyne Art Foundation** (*125 N. Gadsden St.; Tue–Sat 10am–5pm; 850-222-8800; www.lemoyne.org*).

Calhoun Street Historic District
Bounded by Tennessee, Georgia and Meridian Sts.
Called "Gold Dust Street" in the mid-19C because it counted so many prominent Tallahassee citizens among its residents, Calhoun Street still boasts a number of elegant Antebellum mansions and cottages

MUSEUMS

⚓ National Museum of Naval Aviation★★

8.5mi from downtown Pensacola at the Naval Air Station. Open year-round daily 9am–5pm. 850-453-2389 or 800-327-5002. www.navalaviationmuseum.org.

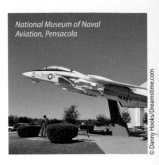

National Museum of Naval Aviation, Pensacola

© Danny Hooks/Dreamstime.com

More than 150 aircraft and nearly 300,000sq ft of exhibit space make this one of the largest air and space museums in the world. Among the many aerial highlights are a sleek fleet of the Blue Angels' A-4 Skyhawks, a replica World War II aircraft carrier, a replica World War II airship, hands-on trainer cockpits, and a Stearman biplane flown by former president George H.W. Bush. Three different flight simulators—motion-based, Max Force 360 degrees, and a Top Gun combat F-14—let you feel what it's like to be a military pilot (*$5–$25 each*). The IMAX theater (*$8.50*) presents a variety of films, including the museum's signature film *The Magic of Flight*.

Museum of Florida History★

500 S. Bronough St., Tallahassee. Open year-round Mon–Fri 9am–4:30pm, Sat 10am–4:30pm, Sun & holidays noon–4:30pm. 850-245-6400. www.museumofflorida history.com.

A re-created Confederate campsite and a replica citrus packing house (c.1920) recount the state's history from prehistoric times to the 20C. Of particular interest is a 12,000-year-old **mastodon skeleton** discovered in Wakulla Springs in 1930. The museum also administers the **Knott House Museum**★ *(301 E. Park Ave., Tallahassee; 850-922-2459; visit by 1hr guided tour only Wed–Fri 1–3pm, Sat 10am–3pm)*, a Classical Revival home built c.1843. Union general Edward McCook read the Emancipation Proclamation from its front steps on May 20, 1865.

Tallahassee Museum of History and Natural Science★

3945 Museum Dr. Open year-round Mon–Sat 9am–5pm, Sun 12:30–5pm. $9. 850-576-1636. www.tallahasseemuseum.org.

This museum, set on 52 wooded acres, interprets North Florida history, nature and wildlife. Follow the boardwalk through a cypress swamp to a natural-habitat zoo featuring indigenous animals such as river otters, white-tailed deer and Florida panthers. A butterfly garden provides food and shelter for butterflies at each stage of their life cycle, while the .5mi nature trail is perfectly suited for a leisurely stroll or nature study. **Big Bend Farm** comprises a 19C Cracker farmhouse, church and schoolhouse.

HISTORIC SITES

Fort Pickens★

17.6mi southwest of Pensacola on Santa Rosa Island. Open Mar–Oct 9:30am–5pm, Nov– Feb 8:30am–4pm. Tours at 2pm daily. $8/vehicle. 850-934-2600 or 800-365-2267. www.nps.gov/guis.

Located on the Gulf Islands National Seashore, this is the largest of the forts, erected by slave labor in 1834, that defended Pensacola Bay and the navy yard. The colossal bastion was acclaimed as a triumph of coastal military defense engineering. Visitors can see both the original fort and the changes it underwent during its 118 years of service. These include the quarters where in 1886–88 the famous Apache warrior Geronimo was imprisoned and "exhibited" as a tourist attraction. The area also includes a visitor center, trails, a fishing pier and a small museum.

Goodwood Museum & Gardens★

1600 Miccosukee Rd., Tallahassee. Visit the museum by guided tour (45 min) only, Mon–Fri 10am–3pm, Sat 10am–2pm. Gardens open Mon–Fri 9am–5pm, Sat 10am–2pm. $6. 850-877-4202. www.goodwoodmuseum.org.

The buildings and grounds that remain from the original 2,400-acre plantation offer respite from bustling suburbia. Fronted by a columned portico, the two-story stucco **Main House** is topped by an eight-sided, windowed cupola. The interior of the house boasts the first frescoes in Florida. A five-room cottage, Rough House, now

Fanny's Garden Cafe, was built to function as the pool cabana. The c.1911 swimming pool has been renovated as a reflecting pool and the 19-acre grounds have been restored to approximate features of the estate's gardens in the 1920s.

Mission San Luis★

2020 W. Mission Rd., Tallahassee. Open year-round Tue–Sun 10am–4pm. $5. 850-245-6406. www.missionsanluis.org.

This Spanish mission village (c.1656) and fort (c.1696) make up the largest Florida mission established by the Franciscan friars. Here the Spaniards and Apalachee Indians lived together for 50 years. In its heyday, San Luis boasted a population of 1,500. Today, visitors wander around a reconstructed colonist's home (known as the Spanish House), the mission church (c.1680), the friary, and the Apalachee chief's house and council house (c.1660). The site of the fort is still undergoing excavation. Throughout the site, costumed interpreters demonstrate period crafts and activities.

© Visit Tallahassee

Mission San Luis

BEACHES

Grayton Beach State Park★★

1.5mi west of Seaside on Rte. 30A. Open year-round 8am–dusk. $5/vehicle. 850-267-8300. www.floridastateparks.org/ graytonbeach.

This small park harbors a gorgeous 1mi strand of shoreline that has been rated one of the country's top 10 beaches. Though not as wide as some area beaches, Grayton offers plenty of room for exploring or just swimming and sunning. A nature loop (1mi) penetrates a tunnel of dwarf live oaks and emerges out past the dunes and pine flats on a trail lined with wild daisies, goldenrod and saw palmetto.

Dr. Julian G. Bruce St. George Island State Park★★

East end of St. George Island. Open 8am–sunset. $6/vehicle. 850-927-2111. www.floridastate parks.org/stgeorgeisland.

High dunes dotted with sea oats and sparkling **white** beaches characterize this 1,900-acre park, whose beaches consistently rank among the top in the US. Brackish salt marshes, pine forests and oak hammocks here are home to osprey, snowy plovers and diamond-back terrapins.

St. Andrews State Park★

4607 State Park Lane (east end of Panama City Beach). Open 8am– sunset. $8/vehicle. 850-233-5140. www.floridastateparks.org/ standrews.

A lovely refuge of fine sand beaches and freshwater marsh, pine flatwoods and sand pine scrub, this park occupies land on either side of the entrance channel to St. Andrews Bay. Fishing piers and jetties extend into Grand Lagoon and the Gulf of Mexico, where flounder, trout, dolphin, bluefish, bonito, redfish and Spanish mackerel abound. Jetties form protected pools perfect for swimming and snorkeling; you'll find nature trails, camping, boat rentals, concessions and a visitor center, too.

A ferry carries passengers between the park and **Shell Island★★** (*see sidebar, below*).

Shell Island★★

Ferry departs from the Jetty Dive Store at St. Andrews State Park. Summer daily 9am–5pm; call for spring and fall hours. $14.95. Kayaks and snorkeling gear available for rent. 850-235-4004. shellislandshuttle.com. This unspoiled barrier island measures 7mi long and 0.5mi wide, with a gorgeous strand of aquamarine water and squeaky white sand, backed by a scrub-covered dune ridge. For the best shell finds, walk away from the tip of the island, where visitors tend to cluster, and wade a few feet into the surf. There are two brackish water lakes on the island, where alligators can often be seen, and a small, protected lagoon for safe family swimming.

THE PANHANDLE

MUST DO

THE GREAT OUTDOORS

Florida Caverns State Park★★

On Rte. 166, 2.6mi north of Marianna. Open 8am–sunset. $5 per vehicle. Visit caverns by guided tour (1hr) only, Thu–Mon 9:30am–4:30pm. Call ahead (850-482-1228) to ensure that tours have not sold out for that day. $8. 850-482-9598; www.floridastateparks.org/floridacaverns.

Wakulla Springs State Park
Visit Tallahassee

This is the only Florida state park to offer cave tours to the public. Its dazzling formations of limestone stalactites, stalagmites, soda straws, flowstones and draperies are comparable to some of the largest caves in the US.

Wakulla Springs State Park★★

16mi south of Tallahassee, in Wakulla Springs. Open 8am–sunset. $6/vehicle. Check website for boat tour information. 850-224-5950. www.floridastateparks.org/wakullasprings.

Set amid lush vegetation in rural Wakulla County, one of the world's largest and deepest springs forms the centerpiece of this 2,900-acre park. Reputed to have been discovered by Spanish explorer Ponce de León c.1521, the spring pumps some 400,000 gallons of crystal-clear water per minute into the Wakulla River. Although divers have plumbed to depths of 360ft, the spring's source remains a mystery. Longleaf pine, beech and cypress trees dripping with Spanish moss surround the river; alligators, turtles and a wealth of waterbirds

call its shores home. Swimming is permitted, and nature trails lace the park. The landmark **Wakulla Springs Lodge** is a restful place to stay, and its **Ball Room** restaurant serves up local favorites like a breakfast of navy bean soup and fried chicken.

Maclay Gardens State Park★

3540 Thomasville Rd, Tallahassee. Park: 8am–sunset. Gardens: 9am–5pm. $6 per vehicle, plus $6 per person to enter the gardens Jan–Apr. 850-487-4556. www.floridastateparks.org/maclaygardens.

This 28-acre garden was created by New York financier Alfred B. Maclay in 1923 and donated to the state of Florida by his widow 30 years later. Maclay planned his garden around winter and spring—the seasons he stayed here. From January through April over 100 varieties of **camellias** burst into bloom (*peak bloom mid-Mar*), and azaleas, dogwood, mountain laurel and magnolias festoon the grounds. Elsewhere in the 1,000-acre park, you can hike nature loops or kayak and swim in Lake Hall.

THE GREAT OUTDOORS

109

PERFORMING ARTS

From the state capital to the state line, the Florida Panhandle offers a variety of performing-arts venues and performances that reflect the residents' generous and joyful spirit.

Pensacola Civic Center

201 E. Gregory St., Pensacola. 850-432-0800. www.pensacola civiccenter.com.

A full-service arena with 10,000 seats and more than 20,000sq ft of exhibition space, PCC hosts big-name entertainers such as Kenny Chesnee and Elton John as well as trade shows, ice skating and other major events.

Pensacola Little Theatre

400 S. Jefferson St., Pensacola. 850-432-2042. www.pensacola littletheatre.com.

In the best collaborative tradition of community theater, PLT has been providing top-quality local theater to patrons for 75 years in the form of musicals, comedies, dramas and children's shows. In addition, the group sponsors acting classes for children and adults. Performances are held in the Pensacola Cultural Center.

Pensacola Symphony Orchestra

205 E. Zaragoza St., Pensacola. 850-435-2533. www.pensacola symphony.com.

Since its beginning in 1926, PSO has continued to grow and expand its musical presence in the community. Its repertoire of formal and informal works has a broad community appeal.

Saenger Theatre

© 2010 by Michael Duncan/Saenger Theatre

Saenger Theatre

118 South Palafox Pl., Pensacola. 850-595-3880. www.pensacola saenger.com.

The 1925 Spanish Baroque/Rococo-style theater has undergone a $15-million renovation and expansion. It offers diverse performances from Riverdance to An Evening with B.B. King.

Tallahassee Symphony Orchestra

1020 E. Lafayette St., Tallahassee. 850-224-0461. www.tallahassee symphony.org.

In addition to its Masterworks series, TSO offers an annual "Pops in the Park" outdoor evening concert series in the spring and a madrigal program in December; there's also a joint concert with the Tallahassee Youth Symphony. TSO adds to the public's enjoyment of symphonic music with open rehearsals, lunchtime chats with Maestra Miriam Burns, and pre-concert lectures on Masterworks programs.

MUST DO

THE PANHANDLE

SHOPPING

Apalachicola

Find material for both reading and knitting in **Downtown Books & Purl** (67 Commerce St.; 850-653-1290). **Richard Bickel Photography** (81 Market St.; 850-653-2828; richardbickel photography.com) exhibits this award-winning photographer's images of "Old Florida."

Pensacola

Pensacola claims two major malls—upscale **Cordova Mall** (5100 N. Ninth Ave.; 850-477-5355) and **University Mall** (7171 N. Davis Hwy.; 850-478-3601). Boutiques, galleries and restaurants populate the downtown Pensacola shopping district (Palafox St. between Main and Wright Sts.), joined on Saturdays by the **Palafox Market** (Martin Luther King Plaza, on N. Palafox St.), where local farmers sell produce and more.

Tallahassee

Want one-stop shopping? Try **Tallahassee Mall** (2415 N. Monroe St., Tallahassee; 850-385-7145; www.shoptallahassee mall.com), but don't overlook the more than 100 locally owned establishments in town. (for suggestions, check online at: locallyownedtallahassee.com)

NIGHTLIFE

Note that cover charges may apply for clubs.

Pensacola

This city's diverse nightlife begins with **Blazzues** blues and jazz band (200 S. Palafox Pl., at the corner of Intendencia St.; 850-696-2290). At **Seville Quarter** (130 E. Government St.; 850-434-6211; www.sevillequarter.com), a larger-than-life entertainment complex boasts seven distinctive venues, each offering a different type of entertainment from music to billiards – not to mention Happy Hour drink discounts. **Vinyl Music Hall** (2 S. Palafox Pl.; 877-435-9849; www.vinylmusic hall.com) shows off a broad range of musical genres in its standing-room-only venue (note that for some events you must be 21 or over to attend).

Tallahassee

As the state capital and home to Florida State University, Tallahassee has a mix of nightspots for both young and mature revelers. **Potbelly's and The Painted Lady** (459 W. College Ave.; 850-224-2233; www.potbellys.net) put two separate clubs at one location. Potbelly's caters to the college crowd, while the Lady's demographic is more upscale. Wednesday night jam sessions make **B Sharp's Jazz Café** one of the coolest spots in town (648 W. Brevard St.; 850-681-2400; www.b-sharps.com). **Bradfordville Blues Club** (7152 Moses Lane; 850-906-0766; www.bradfordvilleblues.com) has hosted many Southern Blues greats.

SOUTHWEST COAST

Stretching about 170 miles along the Gulf of Mexico – from Tampa down to Naples – Florida's southwest coast has everything you'd want from a beach vacation: mile after mile of powdery white sand and aquamarine water, fine restaurants, nightlife, museums, shopping, golf and tennis galore, and atmospheric cypress swamps filled with alligators, wood storks and other critters.

Tampa★★, Florida's third-largest city, has carved out a niche for itself as the state's west-coast capital, while neighboring St. Petersburg is known for its museums and waterfront area. The cities of **Sarasota★★** and **Naples★** are the swankiest, with shopping districts that rival Palm Beach's over-the-top glitz. **Fort Myers**, in between the two, boasts the **Edison and Ford Winter Estates★**, a must-see for history buffs. Though far from undiscovered, the barrier islands of **Sanibel and Captiva★★** bring a measure of tranquility not found on the mainland. Here, finding pristine seashells is a major sport. South of Naples, **Marco Island** and the **Ten Thousand Islands** are popular resort areas. For an island adventure, hop the ferry from Marco Island to **Key West★★★**, where you don't need a car to get around.

Practical Information

When to Go

High season along the southwest coast is roughly Oct–April. **Naples** is substantially warmer than Tampa in the winter, though Gulf breezes make both pleasant year-round.
Hurricane season runs from Jun–Nov, with most activity in August.

Getting There and Around

Three major airports serve the southwest coast:

- **Tampa International Airport** (**TPA**), 5mi west of the city (813-870-8700; www.tampa airport.com);
- **Southwest Florida International Airport** (**RSW**) in Fort Myers (239-590-4800; www.flylcpa.com)

- **Sarasota Bradenton International Airport** (**SRQ**) (941-359-2777; srq-airport.com) All have rental-car agencies, taxis and shuttles. There is no passenger rail service along this corridor.

Visitor Information

- **Tampa** – 615 Channelside Dr.; 831-223-2752 or 800-448-2672; www.visittampabay.com.
- **Fort Myers** – 2310 Edwards Dr.; 800-366-3622 or 239-332-3624; www.fortmyers.org.
- **Naples** – 900 5th Ave. S.; 239-262 -6141; www.naples-florida.com.
- **Sarasota** – 701 North Tamiami Tr., 800-800-3906 www.sarasotafl.org.
- **Sanibel/Captiva Islands** – 239-472-1080; www.sanibel-captiva.org.

113

Sarasota★★

Sarasota (pop. 54,349) offers one of Florida's best-balanced menus of attractions: museums and galleries, chic shopping districts, fine restaurants and bustling street life, botanical gardens, and a 35-mile stretch of superb beach. North of town, the **John and Mable Ringling Museum of Art**★★ is the city's one unmissable sight (*see Museums*). But for Florida charm it's hard to beat downtown **Sarasota**★.

Sidewalk cafes, bakeries, art galleries, gourmet markets and chic boutiques line Main Street. On Saturday mornings (*7am–noon*) a **farmers' market** at Main and Lemon streets brims with fresh flowers, vegetables and fruits, artisanal foods and crafts. Burns Court, a tiny side street, features a popular art-film cinema and bungalow houses dating from the 1920s, while Pineapple Avenue is the city's **antique center**. Art galleries line Palm Avenue as well

as **Towles Court** (*Adams Lane and Morrill St.*), a bungalow colony about three-quarters of a mile due east. Take the Ringling Causeway to **Lido Key** for some great public beaches and the shops and restaurants of St. Armands Circle (*see Shopping*).

The Pier, St. Petersburg

Photo Courtesy of Visit Florida

St. Petersburg★★

Linked to Tampa and its fast-paced commerce by three bridges, sunny **St. Petersburg** (pop. 248,000) is a thriving city – Florida's fourth largest – of young professionals, university students and retirees. Here, in this laid-back community, you'll find first-rate museums, sparkling Gulf beaches, and seven miles of landscaped waterfront that merit a day's exploration. Tourist central in downtown St. Pete is ⚓ **The Pier**★ *(east end of 2nd Ave. N.E.; 727-821-6164; www.stpetepier.com)*, a five-story upside-down ziggurat that juts a quarter of a mile into Tampa Bay. It contains restaurants, gift shops and a small **aquarium** *(727-895-7437; www.pieraquarium.org; $5)*. Head to the **Pier Baithouse** *(727-*

Cafe on the Beach

4000 Gulf Dr., Holmes Beach, Anna Maria Island (20mi northwest of Sarasota). 941-778-0784. Worth the drive for its low-key atmosphere and uncrowded stretches of sand, **Anna Maria Island** boasts many seaside restaurants, and this spot is as friendly and casual as they come. In the morning, order the all-you-can-eat pancake breakfast, served up with sausages and hot coffee. Or come back later in the day to watch the sunset with a Philly cheesesteak.

Ybor City

1.6mi from downtown Tampa. Grab a walking tour map at the visitor center at 1600 E. 8th Ave., Suite 104B. 813-241-8838. www.ybor.org. Named after Spanish-born cigar maker **Vicente Martínez Ybor**, this neighborhood was the cigar-making capital of the world for about 50 years.

Many of the Spanish, Italian and Cuban immigrants who worked in the factories also lived here, bringing their own traditions like the strong and sweet *cafe con leche* you can still order at many coffee shops.

The historic district is now best known for its buzzing nightlife along 7th Avenue (*between 13th and 20th Sts.*), but it makes for a pleasant daytime stroll as well. The **Ybor City Museum State Park** (*1818 9th Ave., 813-247-6323, www.ybormuseum.org*) has exhibits on the cigar industry, a re-created worker's home (*casita*), and a Mediterranean-style garden.

821-3750; www.thepierbait house.com) to purchase bait and tackle, to feed the pelicans or to arrange a boat charter.

From the Pier, it's only a few blocks to the city's most sensational attraction, the **The Dalí Museum**★★★ (*see Museums*), which reopened in a head-turning new building in January 2011. Another recent move brought the much-loved **Morean Arts Center** to the waterfront with a fine new permanent collection of studio glass by Dale Chihuly.

The stunning new gallery (*400 Beach Dr. NE; 727-822-7872; www.moreanartscenter.org*) stands just a block north of the staid **Museum of Fine Arts** (*see Museums*). The Morean's **Glass**

Studio & Hot Shop remain open at 719 Central Avenue.

Tampa★★

Florida's third-largest city (pop. 326,593) is both port and resort. While it lacks the charm of a place like Sarasota, a few sites and historic neighborhoods are definitely worth visiting – and it's a perfect jumping-off spot for a cruise or further exploration of the coast.

The best of downtown Tampa's early architecture survived the wrecking ball and stands today in the shadow of 30- to 40-story skyscrapers; the elegant 1915 Beaux-Arts **City Hall** (*Kennedy Blvd. and Florida Ave.*) is one example. Supersize venues are scattered along the waterfront, including the **St. Pete Times Forum** arena, the **Garrison Seaport Center** cruise terminal, and the **Florida Aquarium**★ (*see Family Fun*). Facing off across the Hillsborough River are the **Henry B. Plant Museum**★, in what was formerly the lavish Tampa Bay Hotel (*see Museums*), and the eye-popping **Tampa Museum of Art** (*120 W. Gasparilla Plaza; 813-274-*

Henry B. Plant Museum, Tampa

© Richard Nowitz/Apa Publications

8130; *www.tampamuseum.org*), which holds more than 400 Greek and Roman works as well as contemporary American art, photography and works on paper. About 11mi north of downtown, the **Museum of Science and Industry**★★ is the largest of its kind in the Southeast (*see Museums*).

Hyde Park★★
North and south of Swann Ave. between South Crosstown Expressway (Rte. 618) and Bayshore Blvd.
Queen Annes and Colonial Revivals elbow Mediterranean Revivals and eclectic bungalows in this wealthy neighborhood. Tampa's most fashionable shopping district, **Old Hyde Park Village**, lines South Dakota and Snow avenues south of Swann Avenue (*See Shopping*).

Naples★
Just west of Big Cypress Swamp and north of the Everglades, **Naples** (pop. 21,709) marks the edge of civilization at the southwest end of Florida. Like a small-scale Palm Beach, it is characterized by fine restaurants and hotels, upscale shops, the 1,200-seat Philharmonic Center for the Arts, more than 40 golf courses and 9 miles of sun-drenched beaches. To see some of the grandest houses in Naples, take a **scenic drive**★ down Gulf Shore Boulevard, continuing on to Gordon Drive, where the residences are larger and more modern. The **beach** near 18th Street South is lovely and uncrowded.
So-called **Old Naples**★, the historic downtown, offers chic shops and eateries that open

Galleries and boutiques on Third Street South, Naples

© Richard Nowitz/Apa Publications

onto palm-lined streets, as well as shaded courtyards perfect for sipping tea or coffee. Galleries and boutiques crowd along **Third Street South**, particularly near Broad Avenue. For other shops, stroll down Fifth Avenue South from Third to Ninth St.
Press on one more block for a historical whistle stop at the Mediterranean-style **Naples Depot Museum** (*1051 5th Ave. S.; 239-262-6525; www.collier museums.com*), where restored rail cars, a Seminole dugout canoe and interactive exhibits tell the story of how trade and travel transformed Naples.

Corkscrew Swamp Sanctuary
30mi NE of Naples. Open year-round daily 7am–5:30pm (7:30pm in summer). $10. 239-348-9151. www.corkscrewaudubon.org.
The country's largest stand of virgin cypress trees occupies this 11,000-acre tract. A 2.25mi boardwalk trail snakes through dense saw palmetto to a swamp marked by soaring 500-year-old cypress trees.

MUSEUMS

The Dalí Museum★★★

1 Dali Blvd., St. Petersburg.
Open year-round Mon–Sat 10am–
5:30pm (Thu 8pm), Sun noon–
5:30pm. $21. 727-823-3767.
www.thedali.org.

One of Florida's most popular
art museums, the Dalí holds the
world's most comprehensive
collection of works by Surrealist
Salvador Dalí outside his native
Spain. The far-out new building
(2011), by Yann Weymouth,
captures Dali's playfully sinister
appeal, with snaking geodesic
glass panels on the exterior and
a spiral staircase within meant to
evoke the DNA helix, which Dalí
apparently admired.
All of the museum's 96 oil paintings
are now on view, in chronological
order, along with a selection of its
100-plus watercolors and drawings
and 1,300 graphics, sculptures,
photographs and objets d'art.
Four of Dali's masterworks, each
of which took at least a year to
complete, are exhibited in their
own salons. These tremendous
canvases, measuring about 13ft by
10ft, were painted between 1948

and 1970. Stay for tapas in the
Spanish-inflected 🍴 **Café Gala**.

John and Mable Ringling Museum of Art★★

5401 Bayshore Rd., Sarasota.
Tickets include admission to
Ringling Museum, Cà d'Zan, and
Circus Museum. Open year-round
daily 10am–5pm (Thu 8pm). $25.
941-359-5700. www.ringling.org.

Iowa native **John Ringling** made
his fortune as one of the founders
(with four of his brothers) of
the Ringling Bros. circus, but his
interest in real estate and art
rivaled his passion for the big top.
A major force in the Florida land
boom of the 1920s, he bought up
property in and around Sarasota,
and in 1927 he and his wife, Mable,
began construction on their estate
grounds of an Italian Renaissance-
style museum to house their
rapidly growing art collection.
It opened in 1931 and was
bequeathed to the state of Florida
upon Ringling's death in 1936; ten
years later it was designated as
Florida's official art museum.

John and Mable Ringling Museum of Art, Sarasota

© Richard Nowitz/Apa Publications

MUSEUMS

Museum of Art

The Ringling's collection contains more than 14,000 objects, among them 1,000 paintings, 2,500 prints and drawings, and 1,500 decorative art objects. The **Baroque collection** in particular is considered one of the best in the US, including four huge paintings (each about 15ft tall) executed by **Rubens** and his assistants around 1625. Other curatorial areas are 17C–19C European and 18C–19C American art, Chinese jades and ceramics, and contemporary art.

Cà d'Zan

Docent-led tours ($5) are offered daily, on the hour 11am–4pm; reservations recommended.
Ringling's lavish 56-room palace, Cà d'Zan (Venetian dialect meaning "House of John"), overlooks Sarasota Bay. Completed as a winter residence around Christmas 1925, it rises five stories, has about 36,000 square feet of living space and remains fully furnished with its original art and antiques. The design was based on postcards of Mable's favorite buildings in Europe; some have called it "Venetian Gothic."

Circus Museum

The largest miniature circus in the world resides here. Comprising eight main tents, 152 wagons, 1,300 circus performers and workers, more than 800 animals and a 59-car train, the model occupies 3,800sq ft and took 50 years to complete. Circus posters and photographs, antique circus wagons and calliopes, and a hodgepodge of other memorabilia depict the old days of the big top.

Museum of Fine Arts★★

255 Beach Dr. N.E., St. Petersburg. Open year-round Mon–Sat 10am–5pm, Sun noon–5pm. $17. 727-896-2667. www.fine-arts.org.

Housed in an attractive Palladian-style building, this museum features a wide-ranging collection of art. The Acheson Gallery displays some of the museum's most notable paintings by French artists—works by Cézanne, Renoir, Monet and others.
The adjacent Poynter Gallery holds a remarkable trove of early Asian art. Other collections include pre-Columbian art, 20C American paintings, and fine examples of art

Cà d'Zan, Sarasota

© Alanrodriquez/Dreamstime.com

Museum of Fine Arts, St. Petersburg

© Richard Nowitz/Apa Publications

from ancient Greece and Rome, the Renaissance, 18C Europe and 19C America.

Museum of Science & Industry★★

4801 E. Fowler Ave., North Tampa. Open Mon–Fri 9am–5pm, Sat–Sun 9am–6pm. $20.95 ($16.95/child 2-12 yrs). 813-987-6000. www.mosi.org.

This superlative hands-on science museum is the largest science center in the Southeastern US. Among the highlights are **Disasterville**, an exhibition on the science behind tornados, hurricanes, wildfires and the like; and **Amazing You**, which explains the mysteries of the human body. **Kids in Charge** is a vast interactive play space geared specifically for kids 12 and under. On the **High Wire Bike**, guests harness themselves onto a bicycle and pedal along a 98ft-long steel cable suspended 30 feet above ground. There's also an **IMAX** 3-D theater and a planetarium (*ticket price included with admission*), and more to explore outside, including a

butterfly garden, a gopher and tortoise habitat and several acres of wetlands.

Henry B. Plant Museum★

401 W. Kennedy Blvd., Tampa. Open Tue–Sat 10am–5pm, Sun noon–5pm (open Mon in Dec). $10. 813-254-1891. www.plantmuseum.com.

Topped with iconic silver minarets and gold crescents, Henry B. Plant's **Tampa Bay Hotel** was one of the most lavish in all of Florida upon its opening in 1891. After Plant's death in 1899, it was bought by the state of Florida in 1904, then put to use as the main building of the University of Tampa in 1933. Today it remains an academic building, with the museum consisting of only a few grand rooms showcasing what fortunate guests experienced at "Plant's Palace."

Naples Museum of Art★

5833 Pelican Bay Blvd., Tampa. Open Oct–Jun Tue–Sat 10am–4pm, Sun noon–4pm. $8 ($12 Jan–Mar). 239-597-1900. www.thephil.org.

Art and architecture are suitably matched in this striking three-story showpiece adorning the Naples Philharmonic campus. The 15-gallery museum showcases temporary exhibits as well as rotating selections from a permanent collection that includes American modernism, Mexican modernism, French protest posters from May 1968, and miniatures. Inside the domed conservatory hangs a stunning 30ft red **glass chandelier** by renowned glass artist Dale Chihuly.

MUSEUMS

HISTORIC SITES

Edison & Ford Winter Estates★

2350 McGregor Blvd, Fort Myers. Open year-round daily 9am–5:30pm. Self-guided tour $20; historian-led tour $25. Other tours available. 239-334-7418. www.edisonfordwinterestates.org.

This fascinating complex holds the winter homes and tropical gardens of inventor **Thomas Edison** (1847–1931) and automaker **Henry Ford** (1863–1947). In his laboratory and botanical gardens here, Edison perfected the light bulb, the phonograph, the moving-picture camera and projector, and the storage battery.

Edison's Home

Edison's spacious house, Seminole Lodge, nestles in an Eden of tropical flowers and trees, odd hybrids and towering bamboo—all part of the botanical gardens the inventor used for his experiments.

Ford's Home

A friend and acolyte of Edison's, Ford bought the Mangoes, a relatively modest cottage, for $20,000 in 1916. Outside, a garage houses vintage Ford automobiles. When the price of rubber soared in the late 1920s, Thomas Edison got to work to find another source for rubber. In the **Edison Botanic Research Laboratory** he discovered that goldenrod, a common weed, produced latex. The adjacent **Edison Museum** houses six rooms filled with thousands of items, including more than 200 Edison phonographs

Historic Spanish Point★

337 N. Tamiami Trail, Osprey (8mi south of Sarasota). Open year-round Mon–Sat 9am–5pm, Sun noon–5pm. $10. 941-966-5214. www.historicspanishpoint.org.

This peaceful 30-acre site illuminates the lives of prehistoric Indians, early pioneers and Gilded Age gardening. Visitors can see the shells, bones and shards of a 15ft-high midden, one of the largest intact prehistoric villages in southwest Florida.
The grounds also hold the largest butterfly garden on the Gulf Coast and the restored gardens of former Chicago socialite Bertha Honoré Palmer.

Model T, Edison & Ford Winter Estates

Lee County VCB/www.FortMyersSanibel.com

BEACHES

Sanibel and Captiva Islands★★

Long known as a paradise for shelling, these popular barrier islands (pop. 6,102), connected by causeways to each other and to the mainland, form a 20mi arc into the Gulf of Mexico 23mi southwest of Fort Myers. Though the winter brings a steady stream of traffic, the pockets of tranquility and beauty that exist on these islands merit the drive.

Conchologists won't want to miss the **Bailey-Matthews Shell Museum** *(3075 Sanibel–Captiva Rd., 239-395-2233; www.shell museum.org)*, and the 6,300-acre **J.N. "Ding" Darling National Wildlife Refuge** is a must-see for nature lovers *(see Great Outdoors)*.

Delnor-Wiggins Pass State Park★

11135 Gulfshore Dr., Naples. Open 8am–sunset. $6 per vehicle. 239-597-6196. www.floridastate parks.org/delnorwiggins.

Punctuating the heavily developed shoreline north of Naples, this delightful park offers more than

a mile of unspoiled white sugar sand, backed by sea grapes, cabbage palms and mangroves.

Fort De Soto Park★

3500 Pinellas Bayway S., Tierra Verde (8mi south of St. Pete). Open daily 8am–sunset. 727-582-2267. www.pinellascounty.org/park.

The powdery white sand and quiet atmosphere at this 1,100-acre park has consistently earned it a spot among the top beaches in America. Take a break from sunbathing to visit the fort, constructed during the Spanish-American War in 1898.

Lovers Key State Park★

30mi south of Fort Myers on Lovers Key. Open 8am–sunset. $5. 239-463-4588. www.florida stateparks.org/loverskey.

Occupying a gorgeous stretch of undeveloped barrier island, Lovers Key encompasses 712 acres of tidal lagoons, mangrove estuary and white-sand beach. Wildlife includes roseate spoonbills, egrets, alligators and endangered West Indian manatees.

The Sanibel Stoop

Dubbed *Costa de Caracoles* ("Coast of Seashells") by 16C Spanish explorers, **Sanibel** and **Captiva** beaches continue to harvest a staggering number and variety of colorful shells, thanks to the way the islands' unusual east-west orientation intersects with the junction of gulf currents. A common "affliction" here is the Sanibel Stoop, the bent-over posture assumed by serious conchologists, or shell collectors. For the best finds, arrive an hour before low tide; tides are especially low at new and full moons. The optimum time to discover the largest assortment of shells is two days after a northwesterly wind. Calico scallops, kitten's paws, turkey wings, lightning whelks, fighting conchs and tiny coquina clams are the most common varieties.

BEACHES

THE GREAT OUTDOORS

J.N. "Ding" Darling National Wildlife Refuge★★

1 Wildlife Dr., off Sanibel-Captiva Rd., Sanibel Island. Education Center open Jan–Apr daily 9am–5pm. Rest of the year daily 9am–4pm. Wildlife Drive ($5/vehicle) open Sat–Thu 7:30am to half-hour before sunset. 239-472-1100. www.fws.gov/dingdarling.

A showcase of barrier-island wildlife abounds here in canals, inlets, mangrove swamps and upland forests. Begin at the **Education Center** to learn about the 6,300-acre refuge and its natural history through displays and videos. Then take the one-way, unpaved, 4mi-long **Wildlife Drive**, which offers virtually guaranteed sightings of water birds and other animals, including alligators. A 20ft observation tower along the drive offers **views** of herons, egrets, roseate spoonbills, ospreys and others. For best bird-watching, visit near dawn, at sunset, or at low tide when the mud flats are exposed. Visitors who want to take a closer look at the local flora and fauna can hike the refuge's 4mi of trails, or paddle the 6mi of marked canoe/kayak courses *(for rentals and guided tours, contact Tarpon Bay Explorers; 239-472-8900; tarponbayexplorers.com).*

Marie Selby Botanical Gardens★★

811 S. Palm Ave., Sarasota. Open year-round daily 10am–5pm. $17. 941-366-5731. www.selby.org.

Occupying a nine-acre peninsula on the downtown waterfront, these lovely gardens display more than 20,000 tropical plants, including 6,000 orchids. The **Tropical Display House**, just beyond the entrance, is widely known for its **epiphytes** (plants that grow on other plants and take their nourishment from the air and rainfall), which Include a large collection of colorful orchids and bromeliads. A paved path outside circles 20 garden areas, including the cycad collection, the cactus and succulent garden, the shady banyan grove and a native plant community. The 1935 **Mansion**, at the north end of the garden, was built as a private residence. It now hosts changing exhibits of art and photography with a botanical theme. Nearby you'll find the tropical food and medicinal plant gardens, as well as the butterfly garden, and the Tree Lab housing creatures of the rainforest.

Marie Selby Botanical Gardens

© Richard Nowitz/Apa Publications

🛶 Myakka River State Park★★

13208 State Rd. 72, Sarasota. Open 8am–sunset. $6/vehicle. 941-361-6511. www.floridastate parks.org/myakkariver.

One of the oldest and largest of Florida's parks, this 28,875-acre parcel stretches along the primeval Myakka River—protected by the state as a designated Wild and Scenic River—for 12mi and encompasses a wide variety of animal and plant communities. Deer and bobcat favor the palm hammocks, pine flatwoods and dry prairies, while alligators and wading birds inhabit Upper Myakka Lake and its marshes. Hiking trails traverse the park, as does a flat road good for bicycling. The Canopy Walk, an 85ft-long suspension bridge, sways some 25ft high among the treetops. Popular tram and airboat tours give visitors a close-up look at native flora and fauna *(mid-Dec–May: airboats 10am, 11:30am, 1pm & 2:30pm; tram 1pm, 2:30pm. Jun–mid Dec airboats 10am, 11:30am & 1pm; no tram tours; $12; Myakka Wildlife Tours, Inc., 941-365-0100; www.myakka river.org)*. The concessionaire at the boat basin also sells fishing gear, camping supplies and snacks (gator stew, anyone?) and rents boats, bicycles and canoes.

Naples Botanical Garden

4820 Bayshore Dr., Naples.
Open daily 9am–5pm.
$12.95. 239-643-7275.
www.naplesgarden.org.

Seven separate areas make up this newly expanded and renovated garden. Highlights include the Florida Garden, home of sabal palms (the state tree) and bougainvillea, silver palmettos, and wildflowers; and the Water Garden afloat with water lilies and lotuses. The Caribbean Garden has both pre- and post-Columbian sections, showing how colonization changed the state's landscape. In the Children's Garden, the serene butterfly house offers a lovely respite, as does the on-site café.

Spectator Sports

The National Football League's **Tampa Bay Buccaneers** (*www.buccaneers.com*), known to their fans as "the Bucs," play at the Raymond James Stadium. They won the Super Bowl in 2002 but have struggled since then. An unexpectedly good season in 2010, though, seems to suggest they're back on track.

The **Tampa Bay Lightning** (*lightning.nhl.com*), nicknamed the Bolts, play professional ice hockey at the St. Pete Times Forum in Tampa. They have won one Stanley Cup (league playoff) championship, in 2004. The **Tampa Bay Rays** (*tampabay.rays.mlb.com*) is the area's Major League Baseball team, playing at Tropicana Field in St. Petersburg. While generally lackluster, the team won the American League pennant in 2008.

More interesting to baseball fans is **spring training** (*www.floridaspring training.com*), when spectators can watch pro teams compete against one another in exhibition—"Grapefruit League"—games in March. Along the southwest coast, the New York Yankees train in Tampa, the Boston Red Sox and Minnesota Twins practice in Fort Myers, and the Baltimore Orioles gear up in Sarasota. For a free guide, visit www.floridagrapefruitleague.com.

FAMILY FUN

Busch Gardens★★

10165 N. McKinley Dr., Tampa. Open year-round daily 9:30am–6pm; longer hours during holidays and special events. $79.99 ($71.99/child 3-9 yrs). 888-800-5447. www.buschgardens.com.

Rhino Rally, Busch Gardens

Photo Courtesy of Busch Gardens Tampa Bay.

This internationally famous zoo/amusement park with an African theme is home to some 3,000 animals, 300 acres of tropical gardens, some of the state's best roller coasters and many live shows – plus themed dining and shops. The **Myombe Reserve** is a three-acre habitat that holds gorillas, Asian elephants, tortoises, and more. In **Timbuktu** you'll find the **Scorpion** roller coaster, which drops 62ft into a 360-degree loop. **Kumba** is one of the largest and fastest roller-coasters in the Southeastern US, while **Gwazi** is billed as Florida's first dueling, or double, wooden roller coaster. Four-acre **Jungala** lets you see tigers up close, climb rope bridges and see live entertainment. The **Tanganyika Tidal Wave** creates a huge splash as it careens down a 55ft drop. Even scarier is **SheiKra**, a floorless roller coaster. **Edge of Africa** is an introduction to the park's largest area, **Serengeti Plain**. More than 700 large African animals—from antelopes to zebras—roam in herds on the grassy savanna, which you can see via a skyride, train, or flatbed truck in what's known as the **Serengeti Safari** *(30min; additional fee of $33.99)*. **Rhino Rally** takes passengers off-road through remote terrain and ends with a river ride aboard a washed-out pontoon bridge.

Finally, **Egypt** holds nearly seven acres of rides, including **Montu**, a spine-tingling inverted roller coaster, as well as a replica of **King Tut's tomb**.

Touring Tip

As with any major theme park, a little planning goes a long way at **Busch Gardens**. The owners, Anheuser Busch, also own SeaWorld in Orlando and Adventure Island (a 30-acre water park across the street from Busch Gardens), so if you plan on visiting either or both of these attractions as well, buy a combination ticket. Buy tickets online no matter what for the best deals. For an additional $44.95–$46.95 per person, Quick Queue Unlimited lets you bypass lines for the most popular rides. If you don't spring for this option, arrive 30 minutes before the gates open and make a beeline for the most popular coasters and water rides, then check notice boards for wait times.

Sarasota for Kids

Sarasota may not seem like a kid-friendly town at first glance, but there's actually a lot here to do with little ones. For a few hours of fun, stop by **G.WIZ** (*1001 Blvd. of the Arts; 941-309-4949; www.gwiz.org*), a nifty hands-on science museum, or **Sarasota Jungle Gardens** (*3701 Bay Shore Rd.; 941-355-1112, ext 306; www.sarasotajunglegardens.com*), a lush wonderland complete with a petting zoo and playground, as well as exotic birds and reptiles. The **Sarasota Classic Car Museum** (*5500 N. US-41; 941-355-6228; www.sarasotacarmuseum.org*) holds more than 100 cars—including John Lennon's 1956 wildly painted Bentley and Paul McCartney's Mini Cooper—as well as a working antique pinball arcade.

Florida Aquarium★

701 Channelside Dr., Tampa. Open year-round daily 9:30am–5pm. Check online or at the admissions desk for show times. $21.95 ($16.95/child 2012 yrs); discounted tickets available online. 813-273-4000. www.flaquarium.org.

Florida Aquarium

© Richard Nowitz/Apa Publications

Connected to the Channelside shopping and entertainment complex in downtown Tampa, this aquatic-life facility harbors more than a million gallons of water and covers 200,000sq ft. The **Wetlands** is a humid zone of cypress swamps, mangrove forests and sawgrass marshes that's home to freshwater bass, white ibis, great horned owls, river otters and alligators. **Bays and Beaches** includes graceful stingrays and floor-dwelling guitarfish. In the popular **Coral Reef**, colorful butterfly fish dart through forests of Staghorn coral and sharks lurk in dark grottoes. **Ocean Commotion** is an interactive gallery celebrating the energy of our oceans, while **Explore A Shore** is a water fun zone. At **Penguin Encounter**, you can interact with the aquarium's newest residents: six African black-footed penguins.

Lowry Park Zoo

7530 N. Blvd., Tampa. Open year-round daily 9:30am–5pm. $23.95 ($18.95/child). 813-935-8552. www.lowryparkzoo.com.

Rated the best zoo in the US for kids by *Parents* magazine in 2009, this pleasant 56-acre animal park is home to more than 2,000 creatures, including endangered species such as the Florida panther, Sumatran tiger and West Indian manatee. There are tons of hands-on activities throughout, from petting goats in the Wallaroo Petting Zoo to feeding a giraffe in Safari Africa. Also on site: a playground; a carousel, mini train and rollercoaster; and a water park. Take a break for hand-dipped ice cream at the new Sweet Shop.

PERFORMING ARTS

Asolo Repertory Theater
5555 N. Tamiami Trail, Sarasota.
941-351-9010. www.asolorep.org.
Florida's premier professional
theater company stages some
15 productions each year, in a
repertoire that includes newly
commissioned plays, contemporary
and classical works, and
musical theater.

David A. Straz, Jr. Center for the Performing Arts
1010 North W.C. MacInnes Pl.,
Tampa. 813-222-1000.
www.strazcenter.org.
Located on Tampa's Riverwalk
in the heart of downtown, the
Straz Center features five theaters
hosting everything from Broadway
series to the nationally recognized
Opera Tampa.

Historic Asolo Theater
5401 Bay Shore Rd., Sarasota.
941-360-7399. www.ringling.org.
The estate of circus entrepreneur
John Ringling and his wife Mable,
now operated by Florida State
University, is one of the largest
museum/university complexes
in the nation. Its Historic Asolo
Theater, offering a diverse program
of theater, music, dance, film and
lectures, is itself a work of art. .

Progress Energy Center for the Arts – Mahaffey Theater
400 First St., St. Petersburg.
727-892-5798. www.mahaffey
theater.com.
Formerly the Mahaffey Center for
the Performing Arts, this newly
renovated gem boasts 2,031
European box-style seats and
bay views. Top-quality national
and international artists and
performances – Broadway shows,
the Florida Orchestra, rock and
classical concerts, comedy and
dance – play to a packed house.

Sarasota Opera
Sarasota Opera House, 61 N.
Pineapple Ave., Sarasota. 941-366-
8450. www.sarasotaopera.org.
For more than half a century, the
internationally respected company
has brought opera classics to
Sarasota, performing since 1984
in the recently restored Sarasota
Opera House.

St. Pete Times Forum
401 Channelside Dr., Tampa.
813-301-2500. www.stpetetimes
forum.com.
The Forum is home to the
Tampa Bay Lightning NHL hockey
and Tampa Storm AFL arena
football, plus concerts by top-
name performers, NBA exhibition
games, USF Basketball and
NCAA tournament games, figure-
skating, rodeos, the circus
and more.

St. Petersburg Opera
Palladium Theater, 253 5th Ave. N.,
St. Petersburg. 727-823-2040.
www.stpeteopera.org.
The excellent acoustics of the
880-seat Palladium Theater in
downtown St. Petersburg sets a
perfect stage for a full season of
top-quality productions of works
such as *Die Fledermaus, Samson
et Dalila, The Medium, La Boheme,*
and *Carmen.*

SHOPPING

St. Armand's Circle★
300 Madison Dr., Sarasota.
Open Mon–Sat 9:30am–5:30pm,
Sun noon–5:30 pm. 941-388-1554
www.visitstarmandscircle.com.
More than 130 stores serve up a
fantasy of fashion in this island
shopping center. From beachwear
to flavored olive oil and books to
gifts for your pet, the variety is
boundless. Kids of all ages should
head to the center of the Circle for
a look at the **Circus Ring of Fame**
honoring world-famous circus stars
and the Sarasota area's legendary
circus heritage.

Centro Ybor
1600 E. 8th Ave., Tampa.
Open Mon–Wed 10am–8pm,
Thu–Sat 10am–10pm, Sun
11am–7pm. 813-242-4660.
www.centroybor.com.
The palm-bedecked plaza
surrounded by shops, restaurants
and entertainment now forms the
focal point of the historic Latin
Quarter, once known as the cigar
capital of the world. Nearby, shops
fill the streets where immigrants
from Cuba, Spain and Italy came
to create a new life. **Ybor City
Saturday Market** (*8th Ave. &
19th St.; Sat 9am–3pm*) offers fresh
produce in a festive atmosphere.

Grand Central District
*Central Ave., between 16th
and 31st Sts., St. Petersburg.
Hours vary. 727-328-7086.
www.grandcentraldistrict.org.*
Just a couple of miles from
downtown, this area has been
designated a Main Street
Community and Revival District. It
sports a bohemian flair with shops

and galleries featuring fine art,
antiques, crafts, home furnishings,
cigars and books.

Hyde Park Village
*1621 W. Snow Circle, Tampa.
Open Mon–Sat 10m–7 pm, Sun
noon–5 pm. 813-251-3500.
www.hydeparkvillage.net.*
Minutes from downtown, this
popular South Tampa outdoor
shopping destination features
an eclectic mix of upscale shops,
designer boutiques, tchotchkes
and trinkets. Live music in the
courtyard adds to the ambience.

Hyde Park Village

Madison Marquette

International Plaza
and Bay Street
*2223 N. W. Shore Blvd., Tampa.
Open Mon–Sat 10am–9 pm, Sun
11am–6 pm. 813-342-3790.
www.shopinternationalplaza.com.*
Adjacent to Tampa International
Airport, this is one of the
Southwest Coast's most distinctive
shopping destinations. Four major
department stores, more than 200
specialty shops, and Bay Street
at the Plaza – an open-air village
of fine restaurants and small
boutiques – make up the complex.

NIGHTLIFE

Note that cover charges may apply for clubs.

Centro Ybor
1600 E. 8th Ave., Tampa. 813-242-4660. www.centroybor.com.
This complex in the city's historic Latin community has become the go-to destination for the area's nightlife. The Green Iguana, Tampa Bay Brewing Company, and the Improv Comedy Theater offer loads of entertainment options.

Centro Ybor, Tampa

Photo courtesy of Visit Florida

The Gator Club
1490 Main St., Sarasota. 941-366-5969. www.thegatorclub.com.
One of Sarasota's most attractive gathering places, the Gator's intimate ambience in a beautifully restored old brick building in the downtown area promises a mellow evening of conversation with a Top 40 vibe to the nightly live music.

The Hub
719 N. Franklin St., Tampa. 813-229-1553. www.thehubbar tampa.com.
This quintessential cocktail lounge in downtown has been one of the constants of Tampa nightlife for 60 years. Renowned for its classic jukebox and the decidedly generous "Hub pour" practiced by its bartenders, this place is the real deal.

International Plaza and Bay Street
223 N. Westshore Blvd., Tampa. 813-342-3790. www.shop internationalplaza.com.
Bar Louie's chic urban style, Blue Martini's selection of 25 specialty martinis and live music, The Grape's array of wines at the bar or in the shop, and The Pub's British feel make International Plaza mandatory for nightime fun.

Jannus Live
1st Ave. N. and 2nd St. N., St. Petersburg. 727-565-0551. www.jannuslive.com.
This outdoor concert venue downtown hosts a wide array of national artists as well as DJs and local acts. Be prepared to stand; seating is available only in private suites, the balcony and a party deck. Shows go on rain or shine.

The Venue
2675 Ulmerton Rd., Clearwater. 727-571-2222. www.thevenue club.com.
It's a restaurant. It's a bar. It's a club. All of the above await you at what is one of the area's hottest evening venues. Club V, the Venue's elegant nightclub *(open Mon, Thu, Fri & Sat, 10pm–3am)*, features several distinctive settings to help you fine-tune each visit.

SOUTHWEST COAST

MUST DO

SPAS

The Grand
2717 W. Kennedy Blvd., Tampa. 813-874-7674. www.grand beautyspa.com.
A wide selection of massage, body treatments, airbrush tanning and salon services here is augmented by a Medi Spa directed by a board-certified dermatologist.

Mandala Med-Spa & Yoga Shala
1715 Stickney Point Rd., Suite B, Sarasota. 941 927-2278. www.mandalamedspa.com.
This Indonesian-inspired holistic day spa is operated by a board-certified plastic surgeon. Emphasis is on wellness, melded with ancient healing arts and cutting-edge technology. Here you can indulge in a Shirodhara hot oil and scalp massage and Balinese floral soaks.

Couples treatment room, The Ritz-Carlton Sarasota

The Ritz-Carlton Sarasota

The Ritz-Carlton Sarasota
1111 Ritz-Carlton Drive, Sarasota. 941-309-2000. www.ritzcarlton. com/en/Properties/Sarasota/Spa.
Living up to its description as an "opulent oasis," the Ritz offers more than 100 wellness and anti-aging

treatments. Among the many temptations are the mother-of-pearl body buff and the signature Sarasota Sea Scrub.

Safety Harbor Resort & Spa
105 N. Bayshore Dr., Safety Harbor. 727-726-1161. www.safetyharborspa.com.
This is a spa in the truest sense of the word. The property's five natural mineral springs, revered by Native Americans for their healing properties, are still central to the program of hydrotherapy used in combination with massage and body treatments here.

Spa Oceana at Hotel Don CeSar
3400 Gulf Blvd., St. Pete Beach. 727-360-1881 or 800-282-1116. www.loewshotels.com/en/Don-CeSar-Beach-Resort/spa.
Inspired by its seaside location, Spa Oceana incorporates sugary sand, sea salt, island spices and exotic botanicals into its treatments. From the Sea Champagne Facial to the Floral Blossom Manicure, it's luxe pampering from head to toe.

Tranquility Wellness Spa
149 Second St. N., St. Petersburg. 727-898-7800. www.tranquility-day-spa.com.
Tranquility's services include multiple massage techniques and soothing body treatments, such as the Marine Algae Wrap or the Indoceane Spa Ritual. There's also a separate spa menu for men.

SPAS

RESTAURANTS

Taking advantage of the bounty of its offshore waters, its year-round growing season and the spice-loving palates of its many Latin and Caribbean immigrants, the Sunshine State offers a smorgasbord of cuisines that vary regionally from north to south.

Expensive	**$$$$ over $75**	*Inexpensive*	**$$ $25 to $50**
Moderate	**$$$ $50 to $75**	*Budget*	**$ less than $25**

Prices & Amenities

The restaurants below were selected for their ambience, location, variety of regional dishes and/or value for money. Prices indicate the average cost of an appetizer, main course, and dessert for one person, not including beverages, taxes or gratuities. Most restaurants are open daily (except where noted). Most, but not all, restaurants accept major credit cards.

Cuisine

Southern US cooking styles prevail in the Panhandle and Northeastern Florida. Look for steamed **Apalachicola Bay oysters**, broiled amberjack (a mild, flaky white fish), fried catfish or Gulf shrimp, hush puppies (small balls of deep-fried cornmeal dough), and grits (made from ground white or yellow corn). Alligator stew and frog legs might also show up on a menu or two. Menus inland and in mid-coastal areas remain seafood-heavy (read carefully as some of it might not be local), but preparations tend toward safe Italian and American standards. Smart bistros, many serving **fusion** cuisine, are popping up as the economy rebounds.

So-called **Floribbean food** is prevalent in South Florida. Often this involves chefs slathering fresh fish or chicken with spicy rubs, throwing it on the grill and serving it with sides or salsas made from tropical fruit (papaya, mango, citrus), along with rice and beans. Other specialties include freshly caught grouper (try it encrusted with macadamia nuts), stone crab claws – a local delicacy – conch fritters, conch chowder, and clawless spiny lobster.

Cuban cuisine is widespread in Miami, especially in Little Havana. Don't leave without trying a pressed **Cuban sandwich**, made with ham, roast pork, Swiss cheese, pickles and mustard. Tart and custardy **Key lime pie** is ubiquitous in the Florida Keys. Don't be surprised to see folks in T-shirts and flip-flops dining even in fancy restaurants here and in many beach communities (but call ahead to check the dress code).

Key Lime Pie

© Stephen Walls/iStockphoto.com

Blue Heaven

$$ **Caribbean**

729 Thomas St., Key West. 305-296-8666. blueheavenkw.com.

A former Hemingway hangout in one of its many previous incarnations, Blue Heaven serves up dishes like jerk chicken with brown rice and black beans. For old Key West ambience, eat in the courtyard, where chickens peck under the tables and cats rub against your legs.

El Siboney

$$ **Cuban**

900 Catherine St., Key West. 305-296-4184. www.elsiboney restaurant.com.

Housed in a brick building on a back street, this traditional Cuban restaurant offers a down-home atmosphere, efficient service, and filling platters of shredded beef or pork, rice and beans and *plátanos* (plantains). Try the rich, flavorful conch chowder and be sure to order a cup of thick, sweet, strong Cuban coffee.

Hungry Tarpon

$$ **Seafood**

Mile Marker 77.5, 77522 Overseas Hwy., Islamorada. 305-664-0535. www.hungrytarpon.com. No dinner Sun.

In a 65-year-old building, this laid-back fish shack features a waterside deck and a whole lot of character. There are some surprising twists to the mains, largely due to the classic French training of the chef, but the biggest might just be that you can bring your own catch and they'll cook it up, with a mess of sides, for you. Lunch is all about fish sandwiches.

Mangia Mangia

$$ **Italian**

900 Southard St., Key West. 305-294-2469. www.mangia-mangia.com. Dinner only.

A wine list with vintages dating back to the 1950s is just a bonus here; Key West's best Italian place serves bountiful platters of homemade pasta with tasty sauces. The popular *bollito misto di mare* features fresh seafood sautéed with garlic, shallots and white wine. Dine on the bricked garden patio.

Pepe's Café

$$ **American**

806 Caroline St., Key West. 305-294-7192. www.pepescafe.net.

Check out the autographed celebrity photos, including a picture of Harry S Truman playing the piano, at this low-key tavern, established in 1909. At midday the vine-covered patio becomes a cool retreat. Burgers, fried oyster plates and key lime pie are all good here.

Seven Fish

$$ **International**

632 Olivia St., Key West. 305-296-2777. www.7fish.com. Dinner only. Closed Tue.

Crowds gather here almost every night for rich seafood preparations—such as sautéed fish with gnocchi and blue cheese—that contrast markedly with the sparse decor. Culinary influences are global, from Japanese to Northern Italian. The Key lime curd over shortbread is Seven Fish's estimable version of Key lime pie.

RESTAURANTS

A&B Lobster House

$$$ **Seafood**

700 Front St., Key West.
305-294-5880. www.aandb
lobsterhouse.com.

One of Key West's longest-established seafood restaurants, the A&B specializes in Maine and Caribbean lobster, as well as in traditional Keys' favorites. Downstairs, **Alonzo's Oyster Bar** (**$$**) offers the largest selection of warm-water and cold-water oysters on the island in a boisterous people-watching setting along the harbor walkway.

Louie's Backyard

$$$ **Contemporary**

700 Waddell St., Key West. 305-294-1061. www.louiesbackyard.com.

Louie's exquisite cuisine is matched only by the sensational setting, overlooking the Atlantic. The menu is heavy on fresh seafood prepared in eclectic ways, like cracked conch with hot-pepper jelly and wasabi. The late-19C house containing the restaurant has been crisply refurbished, but the best spots are in the backyard. Outside tables are at a premium, though, so go early (and make reservations).

Miami and South Florida

The Floridian Restaurant

$ **American**

1410 E. Las Olas Blvd., Fort Lauderdale. 954-463-4041.

Inexpensive, tasty food and generous portions make "the Flo" popular among Las Olas insiders. It's always busy at this 24/7 diner-style eatery, where dining rooms are cheery with poster-lined red, green and blue walls.

The encyclopedic menu includes peanut-butter-chip muffins; around 20 types of burgers; Mexican meatloaf; and a "Fat Cat" breakfast of strip steak, eggs, grits, toast and Dom Perignon for two.

Hamburger Heaven

$ **American**

314 S. County Rd., Palm Beach. 561-655-5277. Breakfast and lunch only. Closed Sun.

A Palm Beach institution since 1945, this old-fashioned diner boasts the "world's greatest hamburgers" and more. At the counter of the always-packed place, diamond- and Gucci-clad millionaires are often seated next to construction workers; red fabric booths offer more dining space. Breakfast fare, soups, salads, cold or grilled sandwiches, and, of course, burgers – topped with everything from jalapeños to sauerkraut – fill the straightforward menu.

🔥 News Cafe

$ **American**

800 Ocean Dr., Miami Beach. 305-538-6397. www.newscafe.com.

People-watching is a 24-hour activity at this sidewalk cafe that opened in the late 1980s to give

Sidewalk dining at News Cafe

© News Cafe

production crews and models a casual place for a quick bite. Everything from French toast to burgers to salads is listed on the extensive menu.

Cafe Versailles
$$ **Cuban**
3555 S.W. 8th St., Little Havana. 305-444-0240.

Near the western perimeter of Little Havana lies one of the quarter's most prominent attractions. Enjoy ultra-sweet café Cubano from a stand-up counter inside or outside. Hearty Cuban sandwiches and heaping plates of food from a magazine-size menu are served inside the main dining room. Most of the rib-sticking dishes, such as roast pork, grilled *palomilla* steak with garlic and onions, and *ropa vieja* (shredded beef in a tomato-based sauce), come with black beans, rice and plantains.

El Rancho Grande
$$ **Mexican**
1626 Pennsylvania Ave., Miami Beach. 305-673-0480. www.elranchograndemexican restaurant.com.

Just off lively Lincoln Road Mall, this family-owned dining spot feels like a roomy cantina. The extensive menu offers standard Mexican dishes and sides, presented in a variety of combinations. For a sampling of several flavors, try the *plato Mexicano*, a hearty assemblage of marinated pork, chicken enchilada, *chile relleno* (green pepper stuffed with cheese), beef burrito, refried beans and rice. There's a second location on 72nd St. in North Miami Beach.

Cap's Place
$$$ **Seafood**
Dock is at 2765 N.E. 28th Court, Lighthouse Point (8mi north of Fort Lauderdale). From there it's a 10min boat ride. 954-941-0418. www.capsplace.com. Closed Mon May–Dec. Dinner only.

Listed on the National Register of Historic Places, this restaurant/ bar is rustic and fun, especially for families. In the 1920s, founder Cap Knight relocated several wooden shacks, floating them on a barge up the Intracoastal Waterway from Miami to Cap's Island, north of Pompano Beach. Back then, the place was a gambling casino and rum-running joint. Celebrity diners have included Winston Churchill, the Vanderbilts and George Harrison. Memorable dishes include the house-smoked fish dip, hearts of palm salad and Key lime pie.

⚓ Joe's Stone Crab
$$$ **Seafood**
11 Washington Ave., Miami Beach. 305-673-0365. www.joesstonecrab. com. Closed Aug–mid-Oct. Closed for lunch mid-May–July.

Located at the southern end of Miami Beach, this high-energy eatery has been a legend since 1913, when founder Joe Weiss began serving the succulent rust-colored crustaceans. Medium to jumbo-size stone crab claws are conveniently cracked open and served chilled with the house mustard sauce. Sides—coleslaw and creamed spinach—are big enough for two. Expect to line up for dinner, but if you're too hungry to wait, order from Joe's adjacent take-out counter and have a surfside picnic.

Café L'Europe

$$$$ **Continental**
*331 S. County Rd., Palm Beach.
561-655-4020. www.cafeleurope.
com. Closed Monday. Weekends
dinner only.*

French doors, beveled brick, mahogany paneling, and gleaming brass lend an air of refinement to this venue. Fresh floral bouquets and colorful place settings add panache. Epitomizing *la belle vie* Palm Beach style, L'Europe serves more than 5,000 ounces of caviar each year. The menu changes seasonally, but expect dishes like lobster bisque "cappuccino," seafood linguini, potato-wrapped red snapper, and roasted rack of lamb. The traditional Wiener schnitzel is a Cafe L'Europe classic.

The Forge

$$$$ **Steakhouse**
*432 41st St. (at Royal Palm Ave.),
Miami Beach. 305-538-8533.
www.theforge.com.*

There's no sign on the exterior of this ornate building, but the beefy valets and sleek cars curbside are clues to the clientele. Thick carpet, plush sofas, stained glass, tapestries and art adorn the restaurant's brick-walled interior.

Soft piano music and candlelight add a romantic air. Considered one of the best steakhouses in America, The Forge serves up a mighty tasty oak-grilled prime rib.

Northeast Coast

bb's

$$ **Continental**
*1019 Hendricks Ave., Jacksonville.
904-306-0100. www.bbs
restaurant.com. Closed Sun.*

A stainless-steel bar and concrete floors contrast smartly with the Continental cuisine dished up at this hip bistro. Entrées get a modern twist – for example, a perfectly cooked filet is topped with Boursin and hazelnuts with an onion reduction – while grilled pizzas and warm goat-cheese salad are popular lighter choices (portions are hearty). Come for lunch Mon–Fri for delicious specials like the crispy tempura fish burrito or the Black Angus meatball sandwich.

Cortessés Bistro

$$ **Mediterranean**
*172 San Marco Ave., St. Augustine.
904-825-6775 or 866-409-
4135. www.cortessesbistro
staugustine.com.*

Intimate rooms with hardwood floors, white tablecloths and fresh flowers exude Old World charm and romance at this bustling, Euro-style bistro. Blue Plate specials share menu space with pasta verde, Minorcan fish stew (lobster, scallops and shrimp in stock, topped with romesco sauce), and veal Oscar. Dine outdoors in the greenery-garnished patio or sample late-night fare and live jazz in the Flamingo Room bar.

The Forge

Photos by Joseph C Parisi/The Forge

Creekside Dinery
$$ **Seafood**
160 Nix Boatyard Rd., St.
Augustine. 904-829-6113.
www.creeksidedinery.com.
Dinner only.

It's hard to believe that a busy
highway is only a quarter-mile away
from this rustic house, set beside a
misty marsh. Beer-battered shrimp,
oak-planked grouper and broiled
seafood platters spice up the
spacious, informal setting.
Tiki torches discourage the no-
see-ums on the outdoor deck, but
you can retreat inside, or to the
screened-in porch for a table over
the water. Kids can make their own
dessert, roasting marshmallows
in the patio fire pit; and live music
entertains diners Wed–Sun.

Denoel French Pastry
$$ **Bakery**
212 Charlotte St., St. Augustine.
904-829-3974.

Patrons come for mid-morning,
made-on-the-premises French
pastries to complement an
espresso or cafe au lait. Otherwise
they order sandwiches of Black
Forest ham or Genoa salami on
home-baked croissants or French
bread. Soups du jour and tomatoes
stuffed with shrimp or chicken
salad are added attractions.
A fixture among city merchants,
the Denoels have been baking
here in St. Augustine since 1966.

Beech Street Grill
$$$ **Floribbean**
801 Beech St., Fernandina Beach.
904-277-3662. www.beechstreet
grill.com. Dinner only and
Sunday brunch.

Vacationers and locals alike can't
resist this art-filled, two-story

sea captain's house built in 1889.
They're attracted by the refined
interiors, the entertaining pianist,
and, of course, the Contemporary
Floribbean food. Chippendale-
style balustrades, marble mantels
and fireplace facades set the
scene for signature dishes such as
macadamia-nut-encrusted grouper
with curried citrus cream, and
flounder-and-crabcake roulade.
Sunday brunch is a special affair
with dishes like shrimp and grits,
and Johnny cakes with apple
butter. Live piano music Mon–Sat
nights and during brunch.

La Crepe en Haut
$$$ **French**
142 E. Granada Blvd., Ormond
Beach. 386-673-1999. www.lacrepe
enhaut.net. Closed Mon.

Graced with ornamental art,
upholstered oval-back chairs and
textured carpets, and four warmly
lit rooms, this pricey, celebrity-
favored haunt ensconces patrons
in belle-époque style. The menu is
rooted in French Nouvelle Cuisine,
though nightly specials satisfy
more contemporary tastes with
offerings like mussels in Pernod
broth, filet mignon studded with
green peppercorns, and lobster
ravioli. The restaurant-cum-bistro/
bar is housed upstairs within a
tree-filled gallery of shops.

Matthew's
$$$ **Contemporary**
2107 Hendricks Ave., Jacksonville.
904-396-9922. www.matthews
restaurant.com. Dinner only.
Closed Sun.

South of the river in stylish San
Marco, chef/owner Matthew
Medure performs daring culinary
moves within an open kitchen and

135

a dining room that seats a mere 60 (the newly opened Lounge, where you can also order off the restaurant's menu, has additional seating). Walls of burnished blond wood rise high above Jacksonville's diehard foodies, who feast on the likes of Kobe beef carpaccio, scallops with chickpea purée, and seared duck breast with foie gras, from a changing menu. A chef's tasting menu and early-bird set meal are also available.

Orlando Area

Le Coq au Vin
$$ **French**
4800 S. Orange Ave., Orlando. 407-851-6980. www.lecoqauvin restaurant.com. Dinner only. Closed Mon.

This small, unpretentious restaurant serves some of the best French food in central Florida. It's the place where rival chefs dine on their days off. The dining spot is named for its most popular, and least expensive, dish; more daring diners opt for the braised rabbit. The Grand Marnier soufflé wins plenty of applause.

San Angel Inn
$$ **Mexican**
Epcot, Mexico, Walt Disney World, Lake Buena Vista. 407-939-3463. www.wdwinfo.com/wdwinfo/ dining.

Looking for a respite from the theme-park heat and crowds? Duck into this ridiculously romantic spot in Epcot's Mexico area (great for lunch, when prices are lower) and let Disney transport you via a (fiber-optic) star-filled sky, smoking volcano and lazy river. (Epcot's El River de Tiempo

ride runs through the restaurant.) After the obligatory chips and salsa, you'll dine on authentic Mexican dishes, like *mole poblano*, that are a whole lot better than you might have expected given the surroundings.

White Wolf Café
$$ **American**
1829 N. Orange Ave., Orlando. 407-895-9911. www.whitewolf cafe.com.

Located in the heart of Orlando's Antique Row, this bistro is named for the owner's white German shepherd dog. The storefront started life as an antique shop, with a few snacks being served to bring in customers and give the local trade a place to relax. Gradually the food took over – namely pizzas, sandwiches, fresh local fish preparations and some straightforward beef and chicken dishes.

Artist Point
$$$ **Regional American**
Wilderness Lodge, Walt Disney World, Lake Buena Vista. 407-939-3463. disneyworld.disney.go.com/ dining/artist-point.

Enter this steakhouse through the stunning lobby of Disney's Wilderness Lodge and you're already wowed – the massive stone fireplace and totem poles re-create the rustic grandeur of a national park lodge. The food, dubbed "northwestern cuisine," doesn't disappoint: the signature dish is cedar-plank salmon served with a confit of artichokes, and the grilled buffalo steak is melt-in-your mouth tender. Wine pairings come from an extensive Pacific Coast wine list. Reservations essential.

Artist Point
© Disney

Chatham's Place
$$$ Continental
7575 Dr. Phillips Blvd., Orlando.
407-345-2992. chathamsplace.com.
This intimate restaurant is a
comfortable change from all the
theme-park hoopla. The smiling
staff is friendly, and they do a fine
job with the restaurant's star dish,
Florida black grouper slathered
in pecan butter with a dash of
cayenne. The rack of lamb au jus
and filet mignon with peppercorn-
cognac sauce also earn raves.

⚜ Victoria and Albert's
$$$$ Contemporary
Disney's Grand Floridian Hotel,
Lake Buena Vista. 407-939-3862.
victoria-alberts.com. Dinner only.
Disney's most luxurious
restaurant (considered to be
one of the top tables in Orlando)
is decked out in Victorian finery
and lavish décor, with a harpist on
hand to boot. A six-course tasting
menu may feature elk, pork belly,
Kobe beef and quail; there's a
delicious vegetarian tasting menu
as well. This may be your most
expensive dinner out in Orlando,
but it will definitely be one
to remember.

Panhandle

Boss Oyster
$$ Seafood
123 Water St. Apalachicola.
850-653-9364. www.apalachicola
riverinn.com.
If you're an oyster lover, try this
long-standing and much-beloved
riverfront eatery, with Old Florida
ramshackle style and just off-
the-boat bivalves. At last count,
Boss served up oysters around
20 different ways. The menu has
plenty else (shrimp, steak, etc),
but little reason to look further.

Capt. Anderson's Restaurant
$$ Seafood
5551 N. Lagoon Dr., Panama
City. 850-234-2225. www.capt
andersons.com. Dinner only.
Closed Sun.
Started in 1967, the restaurant has
grown to accommodate 725 seats;
located dockside, guests start
arriving at 4pm to see the fleet
come in. Its rooms are festooned
with nets, upside-down dories
and dive suits. Top menu items
are the Gulf shrimp and crabmeat
casserole au gratin, whole fresh
Gulf flounder, and churrasco steak.

Chez Pierre
$$ French
1215 Thomasville Rd.,
Tallahassee. 850-222-0936.
www.chezpierre.com.
This big, two-story, rose-colored
house, full of whimsical French art
and provincial furniture, dishes
up worldly cuisine amid the "y'all"
style of regional politics. Tournedos
of beef, roast duck, and trout
amandine epitomize the classic
French fare. Save room for the
chocolate espresso crème brulée.

McGuire's Irish Pub

$$ **American**
600 E. Gregory St., Pensacola.
850-433-6789. www.mcguires
irishpub.com.

This restaurant, known for its quality steaks, blends a friendly, fun ambience with good grub. Housed in the 1927 Old Firehouse, the dining area includes five themed rooms and a ceiling festooned with some 700,000 dollar bills hanging down. The menu is huge, from ale-battered shrimp dishes to pork chops glazed with Jameson whiskey. You can't go wrong with the fried mashed-potato appetizer, followed by a hefty signature steak.

Saltwater Grill

$$ **American**
11040 Hutchison Blvd., Panama Beach City. 850-230-2739.
www.saltwatergrillpcb.com.

When you've tired of beach bars and seafood shacks, head to this upscale eatery and martini bar. The macadamia-crusted grouper is popular, as is the slow-roasted prime rib. The restaurant, complete with a wrap-around bar and 25,000-gallon aquarium, can get a bit noisy; ask for a tiny table in the corner if you're looking for intimate conversation or romance.

Bud & Alley's

$$$ **Seafood**
2236 E. Hwy. 30A, Seaside. 850-231-5900. www.budandalleys.com.

South Walton's oldest restaurant, established in 1986, is a fun, lively place, with water views and fine fare. The rooftop bar is a favorite hangout for tapas and drinks. Below are beamed dining rooms where T-shirts and shorts are accepted despite the white-linen service. Favored dishes include crawfish and andouille gumbo, and seared scallops with grits.

Marina Cafe

$$$$ **Contemporary**
404 Hwy. 98E., Destin. 850-837-7960. www.marinacafe.com.
Dinner only.

Upscale Marina Cafe is one of Destin's best eateries, with high ceilings tiered for great views of the yachts right outside the restaurant. Moet & Chandon can be ordered by the glass, to accompany sushi appetizers and entrées like pan-seared redfish, duck or filet mignon. In good weather, snag a dockside table.

Southwest Coast

Skipper's Smokehouse Restaurant & Oyster Bar

$ **Seafood**
910 Skipper Rd., Tampa. 813-971-0666. www.skipperssmokehouse.com. Closed Mon.

The weather-beaten walkways and overturned boats fronting this landmark restaurant belie its offshore location. Inside, the atmosphere is definitely beach style: laid back and low key.

Columbia Restaurant Ybor City

Columbia Restaurant Ybor City

Crowds can dine on alligator chili, garlic crab, and steamed mud bugs (crawfish) under the stars at outside picnic tables. Nightly, reggae, blues and zydeco musicians perform beneath the Skipperdome's thatched awning, while patrons (some shoeless) head for the outdoor dance floor.

Bangkok
$$ Thai
4791 Swift Rd., Sarasota. 941-922-0703. www.bangkoksarasota.com. Closed for lunch on weekends.
Fresh fruits and vegetables intricately carved into bird and flower shapes, wait staff costumed in native dress, and hand-carved teak furnishings all translate into a serene setting for enjoying authentic Thai cuisine. Favored for its exotic flavors and pleasing prices, Bangkok excels in stir-fries and spicy curries, crispy duckling and a variety of tofu dishes. The most-ordered appetizer is the chicken *satay* with thick peanut sauce; the much-in-demand dessert is fried bananas. Take-outs make great beach picnics.

Columbia Restaurant
$$ Spanish
2117 E. 7th Ave., Ybor City (Tampa). 813-248-4961. www.columbiarestaurant.com.
Encompassing an entire block within Tampa's historic district, Florida's oldest operating restaurant (1905), still family-owned, is a bastion of Old World charm. Linen tablecloths, gracious service and hand-painted tiles throughout set the scene for tapas, gazpacho and Columbia's signature paella "a la Valenciana." Choose a vintage label from the house cellar or try the house-made sangria. Guests enjoy a flamenco show Mon–Sat *(additional charge)*. Other locations in Clearwater Beach and St. Petersburg.

The Dock
$$ Caribbean
845 12th Ave. S. (next to City Dock), Naples. 239-263-9940. www.dockcraytoncove.com.
Join the hullabaloo at this hive of open-air dining on the waterfront at Crayton Cove. The Old Naples institution (est. 1976) has them waiting in line, especially on weekends, for great seafood, specialty sandwiches and "docktails." Start with Bahamian conch fritters or rock shrimp nachos and move on to the pineapple-glazed sea bass or Key lime grouper. Jamaican Red Stripe baby back ribs rounds out the menu's temptations.

Moore's Stone Crab Restaurant
$$ Seafood
800 Broadway, Longboat Key. 941-383-1748. www.moores stonecrab.com.
A Longboat Key institution since 1967, this unpretentious, family-owned restaurant at the north end of the island offers stunning views of Sarasota Bay. Gathering stone crabs by hand in 1927 on the flats of the bay, Papa Jack Moore built the restaurant's reputation for serving the freshest stone crabs around. The family now harvests the crustacean with its own fleet. Presented as combination platters, single plates or sandwiches, the restaurant's variety of catches, from grouper to pompano, are year-round attractions.

RESTAURANTS

Old Salty Dog

$$　　　**American**

1601 Ken Thompson Pkwy., City Island, Sarasota. 941-388-4311. www.theoldsaltydog.com.

This fun spot combines an Old Florida nautical look with the ultra-casual atmosphere of boater hangouts, while offering great bay views. The real magnet is the Salty Dog: a quarter-pound hot dog dipped in beer batter, deep fried and topped with sauerkraut, sautéed onions or cheese. Traditional fish and chips and grouper sandwiches can be savored inside or out on the shady wooden deck.

Old Salty Dog

Photo Courtesy Old Salty Dog

RC Otters

$$　　　**American**

11506 Andy Rosse Lane, Captiva Island. 941-383-1748.

It's easy to feel the island spirit here in this shiplap-constructed cottage. The casual eatery is now houses offers alfresco dining on the front porch or brick patio, or in intimate rooms inside. An affordable menu offers more than 200 items ranging from large, crispy salads and sandwiches of all kinds to steak and lobster. Nightly entertainment showcases local bands well-versed in Jimmy Buffet.

Sharky's on the Pier

$$　　　**American**

1600 S. Harbor Dr., Venice. 941-488-1456. www.sharkyson thepier.com.

Thatched-roofed shelters and sturdy palms sprout from the spacious deck of this popular restaurant, positioned to oversee all the comings and goings of anglers, surfers and sunbathers. The enclosed dining area sports a nautical look and tables crammed with convivial crowds of seafood lovers, who come for the conch fritters, fried-fish-and-chip baskets, gulf shrimp, steaks and baby back ribs. It's a great spot to watch the setting sun.

Bistro 821

$$$　　　**International**

821 Fifth Ave. S., Naples. 239-261-5821. www.bistro821.com. Dinner only.

The interior dining space of this chic bistro spills out onto sidewalk seating, creating an open-air feeling. Facing the bar and open kitchen, one long fabric-bedecked booth promotes easy conversation with neighboring diners. Start with a small plate of jumbo prawns served with sweet chile-Thai basil butter before moving on to a chef specialties like miso-sake roasted sea bass."

Chateau France

$$$　　　**French**

136 4th Ave. N.E., St. Petersburg. 727-894-7163. www.chateau franceonline.com. Dinner only.

This early-1900s house-turned-restaurant features intimate dining on two floors and a wraparound veranda for cocktails. Feast here on such dishes as *poulet* St. Tropez, chateaubriand for two, and cassoulet *de la mer*. Bright floral wallpaper, lace curtains, wood floors and fresh roses fashion an elegant interior, where red-vested servers dote on diners' every need.

Mise en Place
$$$ **Contemporary**
442 W. Kennedy Blvd., Tampa. 813-254-5373. www.miseonline.com. Closed Sun & Mon. Dinner only Sat.
This acclaimed bistro is a trendy two-tier dining room within a 1920s building downtown, across the street from the Plant Museum. Arches and half-walls separate the sprawling setting into intimate nooks where locals dine on ever-changing creative fare, like ancho chile-rubbed shrimp and lemongrass duck breast.

The Veranda
$$$ **Continental**
2122 Second St. (at Broadway), Fort Myers. 239-332-2065. www.verandarestaurant.com. Closed Sun.
Gracious Southern hospitality awaits at this "dressy casual" restaurant, lodged in a century-old, side-by-side house with a fascinating history. Tastes of Dixie flavor the chef's takes on old favorites: Cajun yellowtail snapper with crawfish, Southern grit cakes with pepperjack cheese and andouille sausage, and Bourbon Street filet medallions in a smoky sour-mash whisky sauce.

Beach Bistro
$$$$ **Contemporary**
6600 Gulf Dr., Holmes Beach, Anna Maria Island. 941-778-6444. www.beachbistro.com. Dinner only.
This tiny bistro sits right on a white, sandy beach. The best seating faces the blue-green waters of the Gulf of Mexico and the setting sun. Signature salads include the warm Bella Roma tomato salad and duckling salad with bitter greens. Bistro bouillabaisse and Floribbean grouper (encrusted with toasted coconut and cashews, and topped with a red-pepper papaya jam) are winning entrées.

Bern's Steak House
$$$$ **Steakhouse**
1208 S. Howard Ave., Tampa. 813-251-2421. www.bernssteak house.com. Dinner only. Closed Mon.
Jackets and ties are encouraged at Hyde Park's 45-year-old landmark, which offers oysters and 21 types of caviar as preamble to your choice of six different cuts of aged US prime beef – from chateaubriand to T-bone. These are all served with garlic butter, soup, salad, baked potato, onion rings and home-grown organic vegetables. Oenophiles rejoice: Bern's is famous for its encyclopedic **wine list**, a tome which cites nearly 7,000 different selections and more than half-a-million bottles of wine.

Bern's Steak House

Amy Pezzicara/Pezz Photo

141

HOTELS

As a state that welcomes more than 80 million visitors annually, Florida has no shortage of places to stay. At the top end of the price spectrum, the grand and famous **South Florida resorts** combine modern amenities with Old World service. On-site restaurants and bars, indoor and outdoor swimming pools, tennis courts, fitness centers, golf courses, spas, and even marinas have become standard features here.

Luxury	**$$$$$** over $350		*Inexpensive*	**$$** $100 to $175
Expensive	**$$$$** $250 to $350		*Budget*	**$** less than $100
Moderate	**$$$** $175 to $250			

Prices and Amenities

Traditional accommodations range from luxury hotels to moderate motels. Rates vary greatly but are almost always higher during holidays (especially Christmas and spring break) and peak seasons (Nov–Apr in South Florida; Mar–Nov in the Panhandle and northern coastal areas).

You'll have a tough time getting a typical hotel room for less than $100 a night except in remote areas or during the off season. If this is your budget, consider staying at a **hostel** *(www.hostels.com)* or **campground** *(www.koa.com)*. Typical hotel amenities in Florida are air-conditioning, a workout room, a pool, Wi-Fi and, if you're lucky, a simple continental breakfast.

For a few more perks and more character, consider a **bed-and-breakfast inn**. These are often situated in historic dwellings in residential sections of cities, or in small towns, giving you more of a local feel. Most include a full home-cooked breakfast; some offer afternoon tea and the use of sitting rooms or garden areas where hosts and guests mingle. If you're traveling with a large group or with children, it might be more cost-effective to rent a **furnished apartment or house** than stay at a hotel or inn. Most properties include a fully equipped kitchen with dining area, separate bedrooms, laundry facilities, cable TV, and maybe even tennis courts, and golf-course and beach access.

Prices quoted indicate the cost of a room for two people in high season, not including taxes or surcharges (6-12%).

Online Booking

Rack rates (published rates) provided by hotels are usually higher than website deals. For more information, check with the local convention and visitors bureaus in the area you are visiting, or try the following websites:

Superior Small Lodging Association – *954-895-4777; www.superiorsmalllodging.com.*

Walt Disney World Reservations – *disneyworld.disney.go.com/book.*

Apartment and House Rentals – Two good sites to check out are *www.vrbo.com and www. homeaway.com* (be sure to read policies carefully, as they differ substantially from owner to owner).

Inn Route – *800-624-1880; www.florida-inns.com.*

Everglades

Redland Hotel
$ **13 rooms**
5 S. Flagler Ave., Homestead.
305-246-1904 or 800-595-1904.
www.redlandhotel.com.
Built in 1904 this characterful place
has also served as a mercantile
store and post office. Each room
has its own individual décor,
and some have patios (and are,
accordingly, priced higher). Close
to downtown, the hotel includes a
pub and Internet cafe onsite.

Ivey House
$–$$$ **30 rooms**
107 Camellia St., Everglades City.
239-695-3299 or 877-567-0679.
www.iveyhouse.com.
This c.1928 house, beautifully
turned out with a pool, courtyard
and native plants, is run by the
owners of NACT Everglades
Rentals & Eco Adventures, who
offer guests 20 percent off rentals
and tours. Lodgings include the
main inn, a B&B with shared baths
and a private guest house.

The Keys

Seashell Motel & Key West Hostel
$ **5 hostel rooms**
               (40 bunk beds,
               11 rooms)
718 South St., Key West. 305-296-
5719. www.keywesthostel.com.
92 beds. 10 rooms.
This is one of the best budget
properties – and the only hostel
– located near Old Town. Set in a
residential area, it offers a peaceful
stay, even during Spring Break.
Rooms are dorm style, but private
motel rooms are also available.

Amenities include free Wi-Fi,
lockers and bikes (for a fee).

Largo Lodge
$$–$$$ **8 units**
Mile Marker 101.7, 101740
Overseas Hwy., Key Largo. 305-
451-0424. www.largolodge.com.
Equipped with kitchens, screened
porches, and living rooms,
Largo Lodge's rustic cottages
are spacious, comfortable and
economical; they also have a
few smaller garden units and
one room overlooking the bay.
A private beach and boat dock
offer access to the Gulf of Mexico;
the no-children (under 16) policy
enhances the serenity. Reserve
months in advance for winter
weekends.

Largo Lodge

Photo Courtesy Largo Lodge

Popular House/Key West Bed & Breakfast
$$–$$$ **10 rooms**
415 William St., Key West.
305-296-7274 or 800-438-6155.
www.keywestbandb.com.
Colorful handmade textiles by
owner Jody Carlson and big,
contemporary canvases add to

HOTELS

143

a lively, artsy vibe at this stylish guesthouse. Four rooms have private baths, four share a bath, but all guests enjoy the tropical gardens, dip pool, Jacuzzi and dry sauna – plus a lavish Continental breakfast. No kids under age 18 permitted; no TV in rooms.

Simonton Court
$$$$ **30 units**
320 Simonton St., Key West.
305-294-6386 or 800-944-2687.
www.simontoncourt.com.
Although it's just two blocks from Duval Street, this secluded enclave of former cigar-makers' cottages is elegant and lush. Oleander and hibiscus shade the two small pools. Individually decorated rooms feature Florida pine furnishings and marble baths. Ask the knowledgeable staff anything at all about Key West.

Casa Morada
$$$$–$$$$$ **16 suites**
136 Madeira Rd, Islamorada.
305-664-0044 or 888-881-3030.
www.casamorada.com.
A spa-like serenity sets this all-suites boutique hotel apart from its neighbors. Blooming orchids, bright artwork and terrazzo floors give the property a Mediterranean-meets-Caribbean vibe. The three female hoteliers who run the property get all the small details right, down to the hidden bench by the waterfall and lounge chairs perched at the water's edge.

Gardens Hotel
$$$$–$$$$$ **17 units**
526 Angela St., Key West.
305-294-2661 or 800-526-2664.
www.gardenshotel.com.
The luxuriant gardens that fill much of this walled Old Town compound were once a private botanical preserve harboring tropical species collected around the world. Composed of three restored historic structures and two new additions, the complex has tastefully decorated rooms featuring wood floors and marble baths—many with Jacuzzi tubs and steam showers. Rates include a buffet continental breakfast served in the sunlit garden room.

⚓ Marquesa Hotel
$$$$–$$$$$ **27 rooms**
600 Fleming St., Key West.
305-292-1919 or 800-869-4631.
www.marquesa.com.
Comprising four 1884 Conch houses encircling two pools and a palm-filled garden, this favored lodging in the historic district is listed on the National Historic Register. Breezy guest rooms mix soft tropical colors with Chippendale pieces and West Indies wicker; several of the poolside rooms have sitting areas and patios. The hotel's sleek **Cafe Marquesa** (**$$-$$$**) specializes in Caribbean-inspired dishes with Asian and other international influences.

Pier House Resort
$$$$–$$$$$ **142 rooms**
One Duval St., Key West. 305-296-4600 or 800-723-2791.
www.pierhouse.com.
One of Key West's original landmark resorts, the attractive white buildings house airy, comfortable and spacious rooms and suites, many of which look out over the harbor. A full-service spa and health club, located in a separate building, supplement the pool and private beach.

Miami and South Florida

Miami River Inn
$$–$$$ **40 rooms**
118 S.W. South River Dr. Miami.
305-325-0045 or 800-468-3589.
www.miamiriverinn.com.
Listed on the National Register of Historic Places, this downtown bed-and-breakfast inn was completed in 1910. Located just steps from Miami's Little Havana district, the gated compound is also within walking distance of Brickell Avenue. Refurbished rooms are appointed with period antiques and spacious baths.

Hotel Place St. Michel
$$$ **28 rooms**
162 Alcazar Ave. Coral Gables.
305-444-1666 or 800-848-4683.
www.hotelstmichel.com.
Nestled within Coral Gables' pedestrian-friendly downtown, this two-story European-style inn has a parquet-floored reception area and adjoining sitting room. The subdued, Old World-style décor of each guest room typically features floral bedspreads and matching curtains. Amenities include fresh fruit upon arrival, evening turn-down, complimentary continental breakfast and morning newspaper.

Boca Raton Resort & Club
$$$$ **1,043 rooms**
501 E. Camino Real, Boca Raton.
561-447-3000 or 888-543-1277.
www.bocaresort.com.
Grand dame of Boca Raton, this exclusive property was designed by Addison Mizner in 1926 as the Cloister Inn, and successive additions have retained the graceful blend of Spanish, Italian and Moorish styles. Reserve at the Cloister (the original building), the modern 27-story tower, the oceanfront beach club, the Yacht Club, or get a spacious one or two-bedroom golf villa. Ten dining spots, two golf courses, seven pools, a spa, tennis courts, a private beach, and a wide spectrum of sybaritic pamperings round out the offerings.

The Pillars
$$$$ **18 rooms**
111 N. Birch Rd., Fort Lauderdale.
954-467-9639. www.pillars
hotel.com.
Bordering the busy Intracoastal Waterway, this upscale urban oasis cultivates British Colonial cachet in decor and personal attention. Past an elegant entryway, a curved carpeted staircase leads to smartly appointed rooms and suites with floral bedspreads, armoires and plantation shutters. Pool and patio overlook the water, with its continuous parade of yachts.

Sea View Hotel
$$$$ **210 rooms**
9909 Collins Ave. Bal Harbour.
305-866-4441 or 800-447-1010.
www.seaview-hotel.com.
A beachfront jewel, this upscale Euro-style boutique hotel was built in 1947 as one of Bal Harbour's first high rises. Remarkably spacious, designer-appointed guest quarters show off rich fabrics, wicker chairs, glass-topped metal tables and solid pine armoires. Cozy cabanas rim the Olympic-size pool that overlooks the Atlantic. On-site services include a beauty salon, fitness center and restaurant.

HOTELS

🛏 Biltmore Hotel
$$$$$ **273 rooms**
1200 Anastasia Ave., Coral Gables.
305-445-1926 or 800-727-1926.
www.biltmorehotel.com.

This massive National Historic Landmark in Coral Gables looks like a misplaced Spanish palace, topped off by a 300ft tower modeled after the Cathedral of Seville's Giralda tower. Vaulted hand-painted ceilings, palm-filled courtyards, balustraded balconies and the 1.25-million-gallon pool are just some of the features that have attracted an exclusive clientele since 1926. Personalized service and well-appointed guest rooms with feather beds and easy chairs help too.

🛏 The Breakers
$$$$$ **540 rooms**
1 S. County Rd., Palm Beach.
561-655-6611 or 888-273-2537.
www.thebreakers.com.

A Palm Beach icon, this 1926 mega-resort takes its cue from Italy's Renaissance palazzos, seen in the twin belvedere towers, the nymph fountain at the entrance and the regal lobby's hand-painted, vaulted ceiling. Luxurious rooms are done in light woods, seaside colors and tobacco-leaf prints. The half-mile private beach includes a Mediterranean-style Beach Club with three oceanside pools; there's also golf, tennis, nine restaurants and a spa.

🛏 Delano Hotel
$$$$$ **208 rooms**
1685 Collins Ave., Miami Beach.
305-672-2000. www.delano-hotel.com.

South Beach's minimalist trend started with Philippe Starck's redo of this 1947 beachside oasis. Billowing white curtains—not doors—give access to the lobby, where large, overstuffed Alice-in-Wonderland chairs are installed. More curtains separate lounge areas sparsely clad with antiques, bric-a-brac, and artworks by Dalí and Man Ray. Delano's white-on-white decor and rooftop spa are magnets for celebrities, as is the **Blue Door Fish** restaurant (**$$$**).

The Hotel
$$$$$ **53 rooms**
801 Collins Ave., Miami Beach.
305-531-2222 or 877-843-4683.
www.thehotelofsouthbeach.com.

The Breakers Palm Beach

Todd Oldham designed nearly everything in this renovated Art Deco gem (1936) off South Beach's famous Ocean Drive. A huge mirror-shaped tile mosaic and velveteen couches—block-patterned in rose, green, and gold—pick up flecks of color from the lobby's original terrazzo floor. Blue and yellow cottons and pale wood furniture brighten the bedrooms.

Bask in the sun at the rooftop pool and Spire bar, and reserve a table at **Wish**, the restaurant that serves Mediterranean-inspired dishes (**$$$**).

Northeast Coast

Riverview Hotel
$$ 18 rooms
103 Flagler Ave., New Smyrna Beach. 386-428-5858 or 800-945-7416. www.riverviewhotel.com.
This 1885 hotel, painted bright pink and accented with charming gingerbread, creates a tropical mood with lots of wicker, paddle fans and palms. Antique armoires and floral spreads on reproduction four-poster beds adorn the guest rooms. The adjacent spa and waterside restaurant, **The Grill at Riverview** (**$$**), complete the pretty picture.

Cabana Colony Cottages
$$-$$$ 3 cottages
2435 S. Atlantic Ave., Daytona Beach Shores. 386-252-1692 or 800-293-0653. www.daytona shoreline.com.
These dwellings by the sea date from 1927. Outside and in, the cottages are painted in cool white and pastels and furnished in wicker, with seashell motifs and area rugs on tile. Each cottage has its own fully equipped kitchen, and there's a guest laundry.

The White Orchid
$$-$$$ 9 rooms
1104 S. Oceanshore Blvd., Flagler Beach. 386-439-4944 or 800-423-1477. www.whiteorchidinn.com.
Here, professional restaurateurs keen on accent and ambience operate an airy, Deco styled B&B bordering the ocean. There's a cool, uncluttered look in the individually decorated guest rooms, with touches like Jacuzzi soaking tubs and water views. A swimming pool and heated mineral pool aid in your relaxation, while treatments at the on-site spa run from Reflexology to Japanese hot stone massage.

Amelia Island Williams House
$$$ 9 rooms, 1 cottage
103 S. 9th St., Fernandina Beach. 904-277-2328 or 800-414-9258. www.williamshouse.com.
Edging Fernandina's historic district, this 1856 mansion is the town's oldest. Its museum-like interiors show off furnishings that belonged to Napoleon III and the

Amelia Island Williams House

HOTELS

last emperor of China. Themed guest rooms boast 17C Japanese block prints, brocaded bed linens, gas fireplaces or other lavish appointments. The two-course breakfasts are equally grand.

🏛 St. Francis Inn
$$$-$$$$ 16 rooms, 1 cottage
279 Saint George St., St. Augustine. 904-824-6068 or 800-824-6062. www.stfrancisinn.com.
In America's oldest city, no place exudes more warmth than this three-story, vine-covered inn (built 1791) on a cobblestone lane. Rough plastered ceilings, dark open beams and flickering fireplaces mark the public space, laid out with oriental rugs. Soft quilts, fringed lamps and vintage photos adorn the more modern guest rooms. Gourmet trencherman breakfasts are served, and a wine-and-snack social hour is held each evening.

Casa Monica Hotel
$$$$ 138 rooms
95 Cordova St., St. Augustine. 904-827-1888 or 888-213-8903. www.casamonica.com.
This castle-like landmark was built in 1888 as a winter getaway for America's top-tier families. Its regal features—towers and arches, hand-painted tiles, iron poster beds—will make you think you've landed in Moorish Spain. Decorated with plush velvets and tapestry fabrics, rooms are fitted with amenities fit for a modern-day king, including triple-sheeted beds, feather pillows and snuggly bathrobes. Enjoy a martini and live music (*jazz Fri and Sat nights*) in the hotel's Cobalt Lounge, part of the **95 Cordova** restaurant (**$$$**).

The Lodge & Club
$$$$$ 66 rooms
607 Ponte Vedra Blvd., Ponte Vedra Beach. 904-273-9500 or 800-234-4304. www.pvresorts.com.
Pampering prevails at this sprawling Mediterranean-style seafront complex, complete with belvedere towers, red barrel-tile roofs and Palladian windows. Big, brightly tiled bathrooms house Jacuzzi or Roman tubs and separate showers. All rooms have oceanfront patios or balconies and four-poster beds. Attentive service and a full recreational menu are the order of the day. A lap pool dominates the fitness center.

Orlando Area

🏛 The Courtyard at Lake Lucerne
$$ 30 rooms
211 N. Lucerne Circle East, Orlando. 407-648-5188 or 800-444-5289. www.orlandohistoricinn.com.
Arranged around a tropical courtyard, this complex of four historic residences (1883–1940) overlooks downtown's Lake Lucerne. Each one reflects the period of its heyday, from Victorian jewel-tone fabrics and sleigh beds to offbeat Art Deco suites with kitchenettes. Breakfast is served on the veranda of the gracious antebellum manor house.

Eō Inn & Spa
$$ 17 rooms
227 N. Eola Dr., Orlando. 407-481-8485 or 888-481-8488. www.eoinn.com.
Overlooking Lake Eola in Thornton Park and facing downtown Orlando's skyline, this boutique hotel operates in a remodeled

MUST STAY

1923 building that's decked out with restraint. The third floor has a rooftop terrace where guests can soak up Florida sunshine and enjoy iced beverages; continental breakfasts are served here. Open to the public, the full-service day spa is up top.

Loews Portofino Bay Hotel

$$$$ 750 rooms and suites
5601 Universal Blvd., Orlando.
407-503-1000 or 888-430-4999.
www.loewshotels.com.

Operated by the Loews Corp. on Universal theme-park property, this colorful hotel edges a large body of water like the bayside Italian fishing village for which it is named. Tile roofs slant out over wrought-iron balconies, and many of the plush, spacious rooms overlook a cobblestone piazza. An added perk: all guests are admitted to Universal parks an hour before the general public via water taxi across the lagoon.

The Cabins at Disney's Fort Wilderness Resort

$$$$$ 409 cabins
4510 Fort Wilderness Trail,
Lake Buena Vista. 407-939-6244.
disneyworld.disney.go.com/
resorts.

The ultimate in resort self-catering, this collection of log houses and cabins is complemented by campsites designed for pitching tents or hooking up trailers and mobile homes. Cabins sleep up to six, so it can be decent value for families, despite the price. There are plenty of outdoor activities, and nightlife centers on a nightly musical review, with an all-you-can-eat feast and sing-along; another option is the buffet at Trail's End restaurant.

🏠 Disney's Animal Kingdom Lodge

$$$$$ 972 rooms, 2 villas
2901 Osceola Pkwy., Bay Lake.
407-934-7639. disneyworld.disney.
go.com/resorts.

When booking a reservation at this horseshoe-shaped lodge, ask for a savannah view room, which offers vistas of Animal Kingdom's grazing animals from its private balcony – some creatures come within 30ft. Decorated with African spears and masks, the lobby

Disney's Animal Kingdom Lodge
© Disney

has a stream running through it and a huge mud fireplace. Enjoy breakfast in Boma-Flavors of Africa, a family restaurant; stop for Kenyan coffee in Victoria Falls Lounge; and consider a South African feast at **Jiko – The Cooking Place ($$$)**.

Disney's Grand Floridian Resort & Spa

$$$$$ 867 rooms
4401 Floridian Way, Lake Buena Vista. 407-824-3000 or 407-939-6244. disneyworld.disney.go. com/resorts.
Disney's most luxurious property is a Victorian-era waterside complex set on 40 acres along the Magic Kingdom's monorail route. Once past the five-story lobby—with carved moldings, an aviary and an open-cage elevator— find elegant guest rooms with late-19C-style woodwork. While parents are enjoying the spa, kids can frolic at The Mouseketeer Clubhouse. The French-inspired menu at **Citricos ($$$-$$$$)** includes entrées such as the signature braised veal shank.

Panhandle

Coombs House Inn

$$ 23 rooms
80 6th St., Apalachicola. 850-653-9199 or 888-244-8320. www.coombshouseinn.com.
The two houses that make up the inn date from early 1900 and feature cypress-beamed interiors with hand-carved antiques, rich chintzes and hand-colored prints. **Innkeeping** is warm, yet thoroughly professional; breakfasts are extravagant and fun amid fellow boarders. Porches are equipped with ceiling fans and rocking chairs.

New World Inn

$$ 15 rooms
600 S. Palafox St., Pensacola. 850-423-4111 or 800-258-1103. www.newworldlanding.com.
Pride of Pensacola, this inn celebrates the port city's nearly 450 years of European settlement. An old warehouse in the seaport district was converted to house the two-story structure some 15 years ago, holding the inn and the restaurant/wine bar **600 South ($$)**. It is so solidly built that even street-facing corner rooms admit no sound. A complimentary continental breakfast is served.

Governors Inn

$$$ 41 rooms
209 S. Adams St., Tallahassee. 850-681-6855 or 800-342-7717. www.thegovinn.com.
Arched and understated, the exterior of this hotel near the Capitol resembles a high-end jewelry store. In fact, two 19C shops were gutted to house the hotel, skylights installed and rooms furnished with plantation-style reproductions. Filled by lobbyists during the spring legislative session, Governors offers continental breakfasts, evening cocktails and snacks in the lounge.

Henderson Park Inn

$$$$$ 36 rooms
2700 Scenic Hwy. (Rte. 98E), Destin. 866-398-4432. www.hendersonparkinn.com.
Set apart by its namesake park from high-rise Destin, this adults-only inn sports a shingled exterior evoking cottages at Cape May, New Jersey. Most rooms are large, done in seashell tones, with French doors to a balcony or

porch. Amenities include Jacuzzi and kitchenettes, and a free bottle of wine. Complimentary buffet breakfasts and full lunches are served in the spot that becomes the **Beach Walk Café** at night.

Southwest Coast

Behind the Fence B&B
$ 5 rooms
*1400 Viola Dr., Brandon.
813-685-8201. www.tampa-bed-and-breakfast.com.*
More cosmopolitan than cosmopolitan in its appearance and ambience, this Cracker-style house overflows with early-American antiques, authentic Amish quilts and hand-dipped candles.
Two of the rooms are in a cabin out back that borders a large tree-shaded backyard and swimming pool, while those in the two-story house (shared bath) overlook the quiet grounds. Throughout, the quarters are quite spartan, as befits the price.

🐚 Safety Harbor Resort and Spa
$$ 175 rooms
*105 N. Bayshore Dr., Safety Harbor.
727-726-1161 or 888-237-8772.
www.safetyharborspa.com.*
Built on springs sighted by Pánfilo de Narváez in 1528, this historic landmark is one of the oldest US spas, and the only one in Florida with natural spring waters (there are both indoor and outdoor pools). Its 22-acre setting on Tampa Bay permits views of egrets, manatees and other wildlife. Super-size guest rooms boast walk-through closets, large bathrooms—and a daily carafe of mineral water. Many have patios or

balconies. The **Fountain Grille ($$)** features a short, Mediterranean-inspired menu.

Tides Inn Motel
$$ 12 rooms
*1800 Stickney Point Rd., Sarasota.
941-924-7541 or 800-823-8594.
www.myplanet.net/tidesinn.*
Ultra-clean and simply appointed, this mon-and-pop motel offers rare value. The spacious rooms are sparsely but comfortably furnished, and there's a large grassy backyard that's perfect for pitching horseshoes, playing shuffleboard, or picking oranges from the trees (juicers provided). The pool area is a private, fenced-in oasis, and the famous beaches of Siesta Key lie eight blocks away – with shops, restaurants, boat rentals and a bait shop en route.

Don Vicente de Ybor Historic Inn
$$–$$$ 16 rooms
*1915 Republica de Cuba
(9th Ave. at 14th St.), Tampa.
813-241-4545 or 866-206-4545.
www.donvicenteinn.com.*
Crystal chandeliers, Persian rugs, gilded furnishings and velvet draperies decorate this glitzy boutique hotel within Ybor City's lively Latin Quarter. King-bed rooms feature a private balcony—perfect for toasting the sunset. Continental breakfast is included in the room rate. First owned by cigar-manufacturing entrepreneur Vicente Martinez Ybor, the two-story 1895 stucco structure now includes a 100-seat restaurant and a cigar and martini bar. A deluxe continental breakfast and broadband Internet access are included with every stay.

Sunshine Island Inn
$$–$$$ 5 units
*642 E. Gulf Dr., Sanibel Island.
239-395-2500. www.sunshine
islandinn.com.*

This small, pastel-shaded inn is known for its enduring hospitality and comfort. Guest rooms are light and cheery, each with an efficiency or full kitchen and sliding door to the pool area. The on-site laundry facilities and barbecue grill for guests are extra amenities that especially appeal to families. The inn is located in a quiet neighborhood across the street from the beach and a short bicycle ride away from the fishing pier.

Jensen's Twin Palms Cottages
$$$ 14 units
*15107 Captiva Dr., Captiva Island.
239-472-5800. www.jensen-
captiva.com.*

Perhaps the most laid-back place this side of Key West, Jensen's counts cottages, coconut palms and beach proximity among its most alluring assets. The resort sits right on the waters of Pine Island Sound, where lucky observers might spot manatees, dolphins and otters. The modest Old Florida one- and two-bedroom cottages (and apartments) come with screened porches and kitchen facilities. Guests can hop aboard Jensen's water taxi to explore the outer islands.

Bokeelia Tarpon Inn
$$$$ 5 rooms
*8241 Main St., Bokeelia.
239-283-8961 or 866-827-7662.
www.tarponinn.com.*

It's worth heading off the beaten path to this ultra-luxurious B&B, built in 1914 on the shore of Charlotte Harbor and great for anglers and those seeking seclusion. The handsome living room has hardwood floors, an original fireplace and Indonesian furnishings; a "tropical" breakfast is included. Every room is done in cheerful colors. Guests can tour the island in the inn's golf cart or bicycles and fish from the private pier. You can also rent a boat; the inn is right around the corner from the local marina.

The Cypress
$$$$ 5 rooms
*621 Gulfstream Ave. S.,
Sarasota. 941-955-4683.
www.cypressbb.com.*

This B&B is a surprising downtown find, within an oasis of green across from the city sailboat anchorage. Built of cypress wood in 1940, the two-story house is compact, its interior dressed in art, antiques and various knickknacks. Themed guest rooms overlook the bay or garden. Served in a sunny, bayside space, breakfasts are extravaganzas of fresh-squeezed orange juice, home-baked muffins and much more.

Don CeSar Beach Resort and Spa
$$$$ 277 rooms
3400 Gulf Blvd., St. Petersburg Beach. 727-360-1881 or 800-282-1116. www.doncesar.com.

This flamingo-pink sand castle—complete with turrets and bell towers—is a St. Petersburg area landmark. Carrara marble fountains and Cuban tile floors evoke the ten-story Moorish-Mediterranean-style hotel's jazz-age heyday when F. Scott Fitzgerald was a regular. Elegantly designed in breezy

Florida pastels and light woods, guest rooms overlook the Gulf of Mexico or Boca Ciega Bay. The seafood-focused **Maritana Grille** (**$$$**) provides on-site dining.

Hotel Escalante
$$$$ **10 rooms**
290 Fifth Ave. S., Naples. 239-659-3466. www.hotelescalante.com.
Encased in lush foliage, this Mediterranean-style complex seems more a sprawling private villa than a public hotel.
Yet this sumptuous escape sits nearby the trendy shops of fashionable Fifth Avenue, and only a block from the beach. Generous, ground-level guest quarters include mahogany armoires, spacious bathrooms, and French doors opening onto a garden or poolside patio. Complimentary continental breakfasts, a well-stocked library, spa services and a frangipani-filled footpath make for a special stay. **DISH** restaurant (**$$-$$$**) prepares a seafood-oriented menu.

Longboat Key Club & Resort
$$$$ **218 rooms**
220 Sands Pointe Rd., Longboat Key. 941-383-8821 or 888-237-5545. www.longboatkeyclub.com.
Hidden behind a guard gate, this renovated 410-acre Gulf Coast resort sits on a private beach of sugary white sand.
Extra-spacious rooms and suites with kitchens have large balconies with views of the beach, sea or golf course. Yoga and massage are offered in the expansive fitness center, and bicycles, aqua cycles, sea kayaks and snorkeling equipment are on hand for guests.

Longboat Key Club & Resort
Longboat Key Club & Resort

🛏 'Tween Waters Inn
$$$$–$$$$$ **19 cottages, 138 rooms**
15951 Captiva Dr., Captiva Island. 239-472-5161 or 800-223-5865. www.tween-waters.com.
Framed by the gentle gulf surf and calming waters of Pine Island Sound, this timeless resort is known for its recreational options and Old Florida feel.
The original beach cottages harbored the likes of Anne Morrow Lindbergh and conservationist "Ding" Darling (namesake of the natonal wildlife refuge on Sanibel Island); plenty of contemporary options have been added.
Guests stay occupied with tennis clinics, an Olympic-size pool and spa, plus bicycle, kayak or canoe rentals. Two restaurants and a poolside bar provide sustenance. Check out the hilarious crab races at the inn's **Crow's Nest** restaurant *(Mon & Thu evenings, Oct–Aug).*

FLORIDA

A

Accessibility 27
Accommodations 27, 142
Airlines 24
Amelia Island 74, 82
Amelia Island Museum of History 85
Anastasia State Park 82
Ancient Spanish Monastery 64
Anhinga Trail 36, 39
Animal Parks, 50, 67, 82
Apalachicola 104
Art Deco Historic District 57, 58
Art Walks, Miami 72
Arthur R. Marshall Loxahatchee NWR 68
Audubon House and Tropical Gardens 49
Avondale Historic District 77
Avilés, Pedro Menéndez 79

B

Bahia Honda State Park 47, 51
Barnacle State Historic Park 64
Bass Museum of Art 57, 62
Bayfront Park 55
Bayside Marketplace 55, 71
Beaches 51, 66, 82, 108, 121
Bethesda-by-the-Sea 59
Big Cypress Bend 36, 42
Big Cypress National Preserve 43

Bill Baggs Cape Florida State Park 56, 66
Biscayne National Park 68
Boca Raton 59
Boca Raton Museum of Art 60, 62
Bok Tower Gardens National Historic Landmark 97
Bonnet House Museum and Gardens 65
Busch Gardens 124
Buses 25
Business Hours 28
Butterfly World 67

C

Cà d'Zan 118
Calendar of Events 16
Calhoun Street Historic District 105
Calle Ocho 55
Canopy Roads 104
Cape Florida Lighthouse 66
Car Rental 26
Castillo de San Marcos 76, 79
Cathedral-Basilica of St. Augustine 80
Centre Street Historic District 77
Chokoloskee Bay 42
Circus Museum 118
CoBrA art 63
Coconut Grove 56
Coconut Grove Village 56
CocoWalk 56, 71
Colonial Spanish Quarter 81

Commodore Plaza 56
Coral Castle 65
Coral Gables 56
Corkscrew Swamp Sanctuary 116
Cracker Creek Canoeing 83
Crandon Park 56, 66
Crane Point Museums and Nature Point 46, 48
Cuban Memorial Plaza 55
Cummer Museum of Art and Gardens 77, 78
Currency 29
Customs 23

D

Dalí Museum, The 115, 117
Dalí, Salvador 117
Daytona 500 17, 78
Daytona Beach 74, 77
Delnor-Wiggins Pass State Park 121
Disney, Walt 93
Disney's Animal Kingdom 95
Disney's Hollywood Studios 95
Dolphin Research Center 46, 50
Dow Museum of Historic Houses 81
Downtown Disney 99
Downtown Miami 55
Downtown Miami Welcome Center 54
Downtown Orlando 99
Downtown Tallahassee 105

Dr. Julian G. Bruce
St. George Island
State Park 108
Driving in Florida 25
Dry Tortugas
National Park 51
Duval Street 47

E

Edison, Thomas 120
Edison & Ford Winter
Estates 120
Electricity 29
Embassies 22
Epcot 93
Ernest F. Coe Visitor
Center 39
Ernest Hemingway
Home and
Museum 49
Everglades 36
Everglades
National Park 39

F

Fairchild Tropical
Garden 68
Fakahatchee
Strand Preserve
State Park 42
Family Fun 124
Fernandina Beach
74, 77
Flagler, Henry
Morrison 61, 74, 76
Flagler College 76
Flagler Museum 59, 61
Flamingo 40
Florida Aquarium
115, 125
Florida Caverns
State Park 109
Florida Facts 32
Florida Keys 44
Florida Keys National
Marine Sanctuary 46

Florida National
Scenic Trail 43
Florida Panther 43
Florida Reef 46
Ford, Henry 120
Fort Caroline National
Memorial 81
Fort Clinch State
Park 80
Fort De Soto Park 121
Fort Lauderdale 60
Fort Matanzas National
Monument 80
Fort Pickens 107
Fountain of Youth
Archaeological
Park 76
Freedom Tower 55

G

Gatorland 86
Gonzalez-Alvarez
House 80
Goodwood Museum &
Gardens 107
Government House
Museum 81
Grayton Beach State
Park 108
Great Outdoors, The
42, 51, 68, 83, 97,
109, 122
Gulf Islands National
Seashore 102
Gumbo Limbo Trail 39

H

Harry P. Leu
Gardens 97
Harry S Truman
Little White House
Museum 49
Hemingway, Ernest
44, 49
Henry B. Plant
Museum 115, 119

Historic District, St.
Augustine 76
Historic Sites, 49, 64,
107, 120
Historic Spanish
Point 120
History of Florida 32
Holocaust Memorial 57
Hotels
Amelia Island
Williams House 147
Behind the Fence
B&B 151
Biltmore Hotel 146
Boca Raton Resort
& Club 145
Bokeelia Tarpon Inn
152
Breakers, The 146
Cabana Colony
Cottages 147
Cabins at Disney's
Fort Wilderness
Resort, The 149
Casa Monica
Hotel 148
Casa Morada 144
Coombs House Inn
150
Courtyard at Lake
Lucerne, The 148
Cypress, The 152
Delano Hotel 146
Disney's Animal
Kingdom Lodge 149
Disney's Grand
Floridian Resort
& Spa 150
Don CeSar Beach
Resort and Spa 152
Don Vicente de Ybor
Historic Inn 151
Eō Inn & Spa 148
Gardens Hotel 144
Governors Inn 150
Henderson Park
Inn 150

Hotel, The 146
Hotel Escalante 153
Hotel Place St.
 Michel 145
Ivey House 143
Jensen's Twin Palms
 Cottages 152
Largo Lodge 143
Lodge & Club, The
 148
Loews Portofino
 Bay Hotel 149
Longboat Key Club &
 Resort 153
Marquesa Hotel 144
Miami River Inn 145
New World Inn 150
Pier House Resort
 144
Pillars, The 145
Popular House/
 Key West Bed &
 Breakfast 143
Redland Hotel 143
Riverview Hotel 147
Safety Harbor Resort
 and Spa 151
Seashell Motel & Key
 West Hostel 143
Sea View Hotel 145
Simonton Court 144
St. Francis Inn 148
Sunshine Island Inn
 152
Tides Inn Motel 151
'Tween Waters Inn
 153
White Orchid, The
 147
Hurricane Safety 31
Hyde Park 116

I

Ideas and Tours 12
International Visitors 22
Internet 29

J

J.N. "Ding" Darling NWR
 122
Jacksonville 74, 77
Jacksonville Landing
 77, 84
Jacksonville Zoo 82
John and Mable
 Ringling Museum of
 Art 114, 117
John Pennekamp Coral
 Reef State Park 46, 51
José Martí Park 55
Jungle Island 67

K

Kathryn Abbey
 Hanna Park 82
Kayak Amelia 83
Kennedy Space
 Center 96
Key Biscayne 54, 66
Key Largo 46
Key West 47
Kids Activities, Sarasota
 125

L

Las Olas Boulevard 60
Latin Quarter, Miami 55
Lightner Museum
 76, 78
Lion Country Safari 67
Liquor Laws 29
Little Havana 55
Loch Haven Park 87
Long Key State Park 46
Looe Key 47
Lovers Key State Park
 121
Lowe Art Museum 62
Lower Keys 46
Lowry Park Zoo 125

M

Maclay Gardens
 State Park 109
Magic Kingdom 92
Mahogany
 Hammock Trail 40
Mail 29
Main Street Pier 78
Mallory Square 47
Manatees 35, 88
Manucy Museum 80
Marathon 46
Marathon Wild
 Bird Center 48
Marie Selby Botanical
 Gardens 122
Mel Fisher Maritime
 Heritage Society 48
Mennello Museum of
 American Folk Art 87
Miami 54
Miami and South
 Florida 52
Miami Art Museum
 55, 63
Miami Beach 54, 57
Miami Beach
 Visitors Center 57
Miami Design
 Preservation
 League 57
Miami Dolphins 69
Miami Heat 69
Miami International
 Art Fair 16, 61
Miami International
 Art Fair 16, 61
Miami Museum of
 Science 55
Miami Seaquarium 56
Middle Keys 46
Mission San Luis 107
Mizner, Addison 59. 71
Money 29
Morikami Museum and
 Japanese Gardens 63
Mrazek Pond 40
Museum of Art, Fort
 Lauderdale 60, 63

Museum of Arts and Sciences 79
Museum of Contemporary Art, Jacksonville 77
Museum of Contemporary Art, Miami 63
Museum of Discovery and Science 60, 61
Museum of Fine Arts, St. Petersburg 114, 118
Museum of Florida History 106
Museum of Science and History and Planetarium 79
Museum of Science and Industry 116, 119
Museum Park 55
Museums 48, 61, 78, 106, 117
Myakka River State Park 122

N

Naples 116
Naples Botanical Garden 123
Naples Depot Museum 116
Naples Museum of Art 119
National Key Deer Refuge 46, 51
National Museum of Naval Aviation 106
Nightlife 48, 72, 85, 100, 111, 128
Northeast Coast 74
Northern Everglades 41
Norton Museum of Art 59, 62

O

Oasis Visitor Center 43
Ocean Boulevard 59
Ocean Drive 58
Old City Gate 76
Old Floresta 59
Old Town, Key West 47
Orange Avenue 87
Orange County Regional History Center 87
Orlando 87
Orlando Area 86
Orlando Downtown Historic District 87
Orlando Magic 97
Orlando Museum of Art, The 87
Orlando Science Center, The 87

P-Q

Page L. Edwards Gallery 81
Pa-hay-okee Overlook 40
Palm Beach 58
Palofax Historic District 105
Panama City Beach 102
Panhandle, The 102
Paradise Key Hammock 39
Park Avenue Historic District 105
Pensacola 104
Performing Arts 69, 83, 98, 110, 126
Pier, The, St. Petersburg 114
Pinelands Trail 39
Pinewood Estate 97
Plant, Henry B. 119
Ponce de Leon Inlet Lighthouse 77
Practical Information 20
Prince Murat House 81

R

Reptiles 41
Restaurants
A&B Lobster House 132
Artist Point 136
Bangkok 139
bb's 134
Beach Bistro 141
Beech Street Grill 135
Bern's Steak House 141
Bistro 821 140
Blue Heaven 131
Boss Oyster 137
Bud & Alley's 138
Café Gala 117
Café L'Europe 134
Cafe on the Beach 114
Cafe Versailles 133
Cap's Place 133
Capt. Anderson's Restaurant 137
Chateau France 140
Chatham's Place 137
Chez Pierre 137
Columbia Restaurant 139
Cortessés Bistro 134
Creekside Dinery 135
Denoel French Pastry 135
Dock, The 139
El Rancho Grande 133
El Siboney 131
Floridian Restaurant, The 132
Forge, The 134
Hamburger Heaven 132
Hungry Tarpon 131
Joe's Stone Crab 133
La Crepe en Haut 135
Le Coq au Vin 136
Louie's Backyard 132
Mangia Mangia 131

Marina Café 138
Matthew's 135
McGuire's Irish Pub 138
Mise en Place 141
Moore's Stone Crab Restaurant 139
News Café 132
Old Salty Dog 140
Pepe's Café 131
RC Otters 140
Saltwater Grill 138
San Angel Inn 136
Seven Fish 131
Sharky's on the Pier 140
Skipper's Smokehouse Restaurant & Oyster Bar 138
Veranda, The 141
Victoria and Albert's 137
White Wolf Café 136
Ringling, John 117
Riverside/Avondale Historic District 77
Riverwalk 60, 77
Royal Palm State Park 39

S

Sanibel and Captiva Islands 121
Sarasota 114
Sea Islands 77, 82
SeaWorld Orlando 88
Seven Mile Bridge 46
Seville Historic District 104
Shark Valley 41
Shark Valley Tram Tour 41
Shelling 121
Shell Island 13, 108
Shopping 50, 71, 84, 99, 111, 127
Smoking 30

South Beach 57, 66
Southern Everglades 39
Southwest Coast 112
Spas 73, 85, 101, 129
Spectator Sports 69, 123
St. Andrews State Park 108
St. Armand's Circle 127
St. Augustine 74, 76
St. Augustine Alligator Farm Zoological Park 82
St. George Street 76, 85
St. Petersburg 114
Stranahan House 65
Strip, The 66
Sunset celebration, Key West 47

T

Tallahassee 102, 105
Tallahassee Museum of History and Natural Science 106
Tamiami Trail 41
Tampa 115
Tampa Bay Buccaneers 123
Tampa Bay Lightning 123
Tampa Bay Rays 123
Tampa Museum of Art 115
Taxes 30
Telephones 30
Temperatures, Seasonal 20
Ten Thousand Islands 36, 42
Theater of the Sea 50
Theme Parks 88
Time Zone 31
Timucuan Ecological and Historic National Preserve 81
Tipping 30

Tourism Offices 21
Trains 24

U

Universal Orlando 90
Universal Studios CityWalk 99
Upper Keys 46

V

Venetian Pool 68
Virginia Key Beach Park 66
Vizcaya 64

W

Wakulla Springs State Park 109
Walt Disney World Resort 92
Water Taxis 77
Websites 21
West Lake Trail 40
West Palm Beach 59
Wilderness Waterway 42
Wildlife, Everglades 38
William Dean Howells House 81
Wolfsonian–FIU, The 57, 62
Woodlawn Park Cemetery 55
Worth Avenue 71

X

Ximenez-Fatio House 81

Y

Ybor, Vincente Martínez 115
Ybor City 115
Ybor City Museum State Park 115

Z

Zoo Miami 67